WOMEN HEROES OF THE AMERICAN REVOLUTION

OTHER BOOKS IN THE
WOMEN OF ACTION SERIES

———— • ————

Women Heroes of the

AMERICAN REVOLUTION

20 Stories of Espionage, Sabotage, Defiance, and Rescue

SUSAN CASEY

CHICAGO
REVIEW
PRESS

To the courageous women of the American Revolution
and to the memory of Paula Ogren, a fellow history
lover, who was both an inspiration and a mother to me

Copyright © 2017 by Susan Casey
All rights reserved
First hardcover edition published 2015
First paperback edition published 2017
Published by Chicago Review Press, Incorporated
814 North Franklin Street
Chicago, Illinois 60610
ISBN 978-1-61374-583-0 (hardcover)
ISBN 978-1-61373-831-3 (paperback)

The Library of Congress has cataloged the hardcover edition as follows:

Casey, Susan (Susan Mary)
  Women heroes of the American Revolution : 20 stories of espionage,
sabotage, defiance, and rescue / Susan Casey.
     pages cm — (Women of action)
   Includes bibliographical references and index.
   ISBN 978-1-61374-583-0 (hardback)
   1. United States—History—Revolution, 1775–1783—Participation,
Female—Juvenile literature. 2. United States—History—Revolution,
1775–1783—Women—Juvenile literature. 3. Women—United States—
History—18th century—Juvenile literature. I. Title.
   E276.C37 2015
   973.308—dc23
                        2014032760

Cover and interior design: Sarah Olson

Front cover photos: (top) Dicey Langston protects her father, *Pioneer
Mothers of America* (1912); (bottom, left to right) Esther Reed, painting
by Charles Willson Peale, Wikimedia Commons; Penelope Barker,
photo by Eric N. Blevins of painting held at the Cupola House, used
with permission of 1758 Cupola House Association, courtesy of NC
Museum of History; Sarah Franklin Bache, painting by John Hoppner,
Wikimedia Commons; Phillis Wheatley, Library of Congress

Printed in the United States of America

Contents

PART THREE: SABOTEURS

PART FOUR: SOLDIERS AND DEFENDERS OF THE HOME FRONT

PART FIVE: LEGENDARY LADIES

Author's Note

Women of every age and economic level participated in the American Revolution. The war engulfed their lives as it did the lives of their grandfathers, fathers, husbands, and sons. Some women supported the Revolution. Others eschewed it. Loyalties were split in families, in cities and towns.

When men enlisted to fight, some women went with them. Others stayed home to care for their children and family members, to defend their homes, or to run their family farms or businesses.

Many women, like their male counterparts, were disgruntled when the policies of the British government began to change, and protested when what they felt were unfair taxes were imposed. Some melted pewter dishes to mold bullets, and some made cartridges. Others spun and wove cloth in support of the boycott of British goods, and drank alternatives to British tea.

In the eight long years of the American Revolution, many different battles took place on sea and land in different colonies, on farms and in fields, in cities and towns, in the form of formal battles, small conflicts, or individual incidents between neighbors.

In many cases, women didn't have to rush to war. The war surrounded them, engulfed their lives. Some women stepped up in battles, rescued and nursed soldiers, cooked and presented food, or provided clothing. For some women, their own homes were the battlefields. They acted to protect their children or possessions. Other women fought by acting as couriers, speaking their minds, using their pens as weapons, or printing the news. Still others deviously delayed or defied enemy troops.

Some women left diaries and letters detailing their experiences. Stories of others who could neither read nor write will never be told. Yet other stories of brave women have been passed down by word of mouth in families or preserved in journals and letters or in accounts by soldiers, writers of the time, or historians. A few of those stories are in the pages that follow.

While doing research about the stories, I was alternately awed, shocked, surprised, saddened, and intrigued by the heroic women who took action during the American Revolution. Yet I was also stymied when reading varying accounts of the same stories and events that were incomplete, different, or even conflicting. The challenge in writing about women of the American Revolution, and doing them justice, has been to align the conflicting stories and to separate fact from fiction or exaggeration.

What was it like for women to live through the American Revolution? In what ways were they heroic? Read on. I hope their stories will give you a glimpse.

The American Revolution

The American Revolution didn't start quickly. Since 1607 when Jamestown, the first English settlement in America, was established, colonists considered themselves English citizens, loyal to the English crown. By the 1770s, the eve of the American Revolution, many people living in America had never even been to England, yet they still considered themselves English subjects.

As more restrictions were imposed by King George III—barring colonists from settling west of the Appalachian Mountains and taxing them to pay for a foreign war—colonists began to protest. Resistance turned into action with the Boston Tea Party, during which Bostonians dressed as Native Americans dumped hundreds of crates of British tea into Boston Harbor in December 1773. In the next year, 56 delegates from 12 colonies (except Georgia) formed the First Continental Congress, a government of the colonies, and called for a boycott of British goods.

While many people wanted to fight the British and every family had weapons, fighting against the well-trained British

Army seemed overwhelming. Resistance was aimed at resolving the conflict, not breaking away.

Then, when the British sent troops to Lexington on their way to Concord, where colonists had stored military supplies they might need in case of a conflict, everything changed. British troops faced off with American men on Lexington Green in 1775. As troops were asked to dismiss, a shot was fired. Soldiers were killed and wounded. To this day, no one knows who shot first, but that one shot started it all. Ralph Waldo Emerson in his poem "Concord Hymn" famously called it "the shot heard round the world." The American Revolution was on.

The British sent armies and ships sporting dozens of cannons to blockade the coast and quell the uprising, and took control of Boston.

Colonists were split. Many wanted to remain loyal to the king. They were called loyalists or Tories. Others were adamant in demanding an independent America. They were called Whigs. Others were neutral.

The Second Continental Congress met, created the official Continental Army, and selected George Washington as commander in chief. On July 4, 1776, it issued the Declaration of Independence.

The British lost control in Boston in 1776 but took control in New York that same year and occupied it for the duration of the war.

Cleverly planned American wins at Trenton in late 1776 and Princeton, New Jersey, in early 1777 boosted morale and confidence in George Washington as commander. Britain proved tough to defeat, though, as their forces won battles in Pennsylvania, which led to the occupation of Philadelphia in 1777. Then a victory by American forces in Saratoga, New York, which halted additional British forces from traveling south, prompted the French to ally with the American forces and contribute their navy to aid the defense.

In 1778 fighting shifted to the South, where the British captured Georgia and, in 1780, after repeated attempts, took control of Charleston, the capital city of South Carolina, and defeated American troops at Camden, South Carolina. American militia fought back using guerilla warfare, hiding in swamps and forests throughout the backcountry and disrupting supply lines that prevented the British from gaining complete control. At the Battle of Yorktown in 1781, British forces couldn't defeat the combined American and French forces and surrendered. British troops left America, but small conflicts continued between loyalists and Whigs for about a year while the peace terms were being negotiated in Paris. The signing of the Peace of Paris took place on September 3, 1783, and officially ended the American Revolution. A people fought for independence and to create a democratic nation based on the rule of law and the guarantee of certain human rights. And so began the United States of America.

Part One

RESISTERS, SUPPORTERS, AND RESCUERS

Penelope Barker

◆◆◆

STEEPING THE BREW

In 1774, before the start of the Revolution, Penelope Barker, a charming and capable woman, was the leader of one of the first women's political actions in the American colonies: the Edenton Tea Party.

Edenton, a town of only 15 streets and about 500 residents, was, according to *The Historic Tea-Party of Edenton, October 25th, 1774*, "charming in its refinement and culture" and had been earlier in the century (1722–1743) the colonial capital of North Carolina.

At that time, tea parties were "one of the most fashionable modes of entertaining" in Edenton. After drinking tea, "the ladies would gossip and spin, and reel [dance]" while the gentlemen would smoke their long-stemmed pipes and "discuss the political issues of the day."

By August 1774, though, the Edenton men, like men across the North Carolina colony, announced their protest of what they viewed as unfair tax acts on English tea and also their support of a boycott of British imports including English tea. They

Penelope Barker. *Photo by Eric N. Blevins, of painting held at the Cupola House, used with permission of 1758 Cupola House Association, courtesy of NC Museum of History*

gathered on August 4 for the first provincial convention and voted that they wouldn't buy British tea or cloth until what they viewed as unfair taxes were repealed.

Penelope Barker, called "one of those lofty, intrepid, high-born women peculiarly fitted by nature to lead," took note of the men's

The Edenton Teapot commemorates the Edenton Tea Party.
Courtesy of the Edenton Historical Commission

actions and decided to circulate a petition to support their vote and ask other Edenton women to sign it as well. She was by then seasoned by her experiences and "a brilliant conversationalist."

The Edenton women she approached were as experienced and world-wise as she. Elizabeth King, who lived in a Colonial Avenue home that was edged by creeks and faced the court-house green, was the wife of a prominent merchant. Another signer was Winifred Wiggins Hoskins, who, after marrying Richard Hoskins, a patriot (one who rebelled against British control over the colonies), had traveled with him to Edenton on an open boat down the Roanoke River. Then together they had mounted his horse and ridden along paths and through trees to Richard's farm, which the two called Paradise. Another was Miss Isabella Johnston, the fiancée of Joseph Hewes, who two years later would sign the Declaration of Independence for North Carolina.

Did Penelope approach each woman to ask if she would sign a petition to boycott British goods? How Penelope organized the effort is not known. Many versions of the story note that the ladies met for a tea party at the home of Elizabeth King, yet plans of her home reveal that it couldn't accommodate that many guests. (The notion that the ladies met and signed a petition at the tea party arose after a cartoon depicting the women at a tea party appeared in a London publication.) Perhaps Penelope or Penelope and Elizabeth organized tea parties for small groups in their homes or perhaps visited women at their own homes. However it happened, Penelope organized the effort and presented the underlying topic to the women: how can Edenton women participate in the stirring colonial revolution? Fifty-one Edenton women decided to sign a petition agreeing to stop buying English tea or clothes until what they felt were unfair tax acts were repealed. They also vowed to spin their own yarn and weave their own cloth as had women in other colonies. Thereafter, the ladies drank alternative forms of tea, including one type made by steeping the leaves of a raspberry vine.

The petition reads:

Edenton, North Carolina, Oct. 25, 1774
As we cannot be indifferent on any occasion that appears nearly to affect the peace and happiness of our country, and as it has been thought necessary, for the public good, to enter into several particular resolves by a meeting of Members deputed from the whole Province, it is a duty which we owe, not only to our near and dear connections who have concurred in them, but to ourselves who are essentially interested in their welfare,

to do every thing as far as lies in our power to testify our sincere adherence to the same; and we do therefore accordingly subscribe this paper, as a witness of our fixed intention and solemn determination to do so.

The petition doesn't mention tea. It does mention "our near and dear connections." They were speaking of their husbands. The petition also states that they wanted to "do every thing as far as lies in our power to testify our sincere adherence to the same"—the same boycott as their husbands had agreed to two months prior.

While many women in the colonies had agreed to boycott English goods, the Edenton women went further. By writing and signing their own petition, vowing to support their husbands' boycott, they boldly and publicly asserted their right to their own voice in policy matters that affected the common good, the first American women on record to do so.

Who was the woman who engineered this political tea party? Who was Penelope Barker? She was born Penelope Pagett in Edenton on June 17, 1728, the daughter of Samuel Pagett, a physician and a planter, and Elizabeth Blount, herself the daughter of a planter. When she was in her teens, after her father and older sister, also named Elizabeth, died in the same year, it fell to Penelope to manage her sister's household and care for her three children. Not long after, she married her sister's widower, John Hodgson. By age 19, she had given birth to one son, Samuel, and was expecting another when John unexpectedly died.

Penelope struggled with the responsibilities of raising her five children and managing John's estate. When she was 21, the court, asserting that she wasn't caring for the children in terms of education and guidance, threatened to take both the children and the property away from her. Her family stepped in. Her uncle paid some of her debts, and other family supported her in the care of the children.

In spite of her challenges, Penelope persisted, learned about finances, and managed to purchase six commercial lots on Broad Street, a main street in Edenton, from James Craven, a local planter and political leader. Then she married him. Two years later James died and Penelope inherited his estate. She was 27.

A third marriage, to Edenton's Thomas Barker—a widower, attorney, and member of the assembly who was 16 years her senior—lasted longer, but all three of their children died before reaching the age of 10. As a commercial agent of the North Carolina colony, Thomas was often away in London for long stretches of time, and Penelope managed his two plantations and other property. During those years, Penelope emerged as "a society leader of her day" and became the hostess of Edenton's most infamous tea party.

News of the Edenton ladies' petition was published in colony after colony. The petition and a letter were sent to London anonymously and appeared on January 16, 1775, in the *Morning Chronicle and London Advertiser*. The letter read:

> The Provincial Deputies of North Carolina having resolved not to drink any more tea, nor wear any more British cloth, & c. many ladies of this Province have determined to give a memorable proof of their patriotism, and have accordingly entered into the following honorable and spirited association. I send it to you, to shew your fair countrywomen, how zealously and

faithfully American ladies follow the laudable example of their husbands, and what opposition your Ministers may expect to receive from a people thus firmly united against them.

How was the news received in England? With laughter and sarcasm!

London resident Arthur Iredell wrote the following letter to his brother James Iredell, one of Edenton's leading patriots. Their sister was one of the signers.

London Queen Square, January 31, 1775

DEAR BROTHER:

I see by the newspaper the Edenton ladies have signalized themselves by their protest against tea drinking. The name of Johnston I see among others; are any of my sister's relations patriotic heroines? Is there a female congress at Edenton too? I hope not, for we Englishmen are afraid of the male congress, but if the ladies, who have ever since the Amazonian era been esteemed the most formidable enemies; if they, I say, should attack us, the most fatal consequence is to be dreaded. So dextrous in the handling of a dart, each wound they give is mortal; whilst we, so unhappily formed by nature, the more we strive to conquer them, the more we are conquered. The Edenton ladies, conscious, I suppose, of this superiority on their side, by a former experience, are willing I imagine, to crush us into atoms by their omnipotency; the only security on our side to prevent the impending ruin, that I can perceive, is the probability that there are but few places in America which possess so much female artillery as Edenton.

Pray let me know all the particulars when you favor me with a letter.

Your most affectionate friend and brother,
ARTHUR IREDELL

Arthur asked sarcastically, "Is there a female congress at Edenton too? I hope not." He was referring to the ruling body of

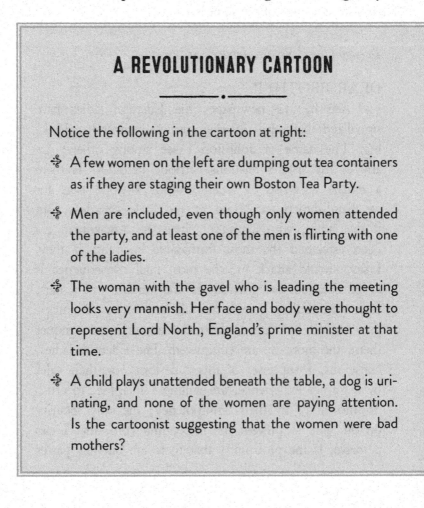

A REVOLUTIONARY CARTOON

Notice the following in the cartoon at right:

- ❧ A few women on the left are dumping out tea containers as if they are staging their own Boston Tea Party.

- ❧ Men are included, even though only women attended the party, and at least one of the men is flirting with one of the ladies.

- ❧ The woman with the gavel who is leading the meeting looks very mannish. Her face and body were thought to represent Lord North, England's prime minister at that time.

- ❧ A child plays unattended beneath the table, a dog is urinating, and none of the women are paying attention. Is the cartoonist suggesting that the women were bad mothers?

the colonies, the Continental Congress, then saluted in Edenton for possessing women who "are willing to crush us into atoms."

All of London was witness to such mockery in the form of a widely circulated political cartoon published there in March 1775.

During and after the war years, Penelope's strong will persisted despite setbacks. As a result of the British blockade of American ports, her husband, Thomas, was prevented from returning home from England and was away before and during

"A Society of Patriotic Ladies, at Edenton, in North Carolina."
Library of Congress LC-DIG-ppmsca-19468

the early years of the Revolution. When the Continental Congress began requiring landowners to sign oaths of allegiance to the patriot cause, Penelope was at risk of losing all of their property. Why? Married women didn't have the legal right to take oaths, and her husband was not there to sign. Fortunately for her, he was able to arrange for a pass from the ambassador from the court of the king of Spain to leave England. Thomas had been gone for 17 years when he and Penelope were reunited.

In 1782 Thomas and Penelope built what is still called the Barker House. He died in 1789, leaving her property in town and two plantations, carriages and horses, and many chairs and books. Penelope lived another seven years until 1796 and was buried alongside him in a family graveyard near Edenton.

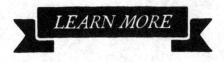

LEARN MORE

Edenton Historical Commission
http://ehcnc.org

"Penelope Barker (1728–1796)"
National Women's History Museum
www.nwhm.org/education-resources/biography/biographies
/penelope-barker

"Edenton Tea Party: An American First"
North Carolina History Project
www.northcarolinahistory.org/commentary/20/entry

Visit Edenton
www.visitedenton.com

THE 51 SIGNERS OF THE EDENTON TEA PARTY PETITION

————————•————————

Anne Anderson
Penelope Barker
Sarah Beasley
Elizabeth Beasely
Ruth Benbury
Lydia Bennet
Jean Blair
Mary Blount
Rebecca Bondfield
Lydia Bonner
Mary Bonner
Margaret Cathcart
Abigale Charlton
Grace Clayton
Elizabeth Creacy
Mary Creacy
Mary Creacy
Elizabeth Crickett
Tresia Cunningham
Penelope Dawson
Elizabeth Green
Anne Hall
Frances Hall
Anne Haughton
Sarah Hoskins
Anne Horniblow

Sarah Howe
Sarah Howcott
Mary Hunter
Elizabeth Johnston
Anne Johnstone
F. Johnstone
Mary Jones
Mary Littedle
Sarah Littlejohn
Sarah Mathews
Elizabeth P. Ormond
M. Payne
Elizabeth Patterson
Margaret Pearson
Mary Ramsay
Elizabeth Roberts
Elizabeth Roberts
Elizabeth Roberts
Elizabeth Vail
Elizabeth Vail
Susannah Vail
Sarah Valentine
Marion Wells
Jane Wellwood
Mary Woolard

Phillis Wheatley

❖❖❖

THE SLAVE WHO PROCLAIMED
A REVOLUTION

One summer day in Boston in 1761, John Wheatley, a prosperous merchant, and his wife, Susanna, arrived at a slave auction at Beach Street wharf. The *Phillis*, a slave ship that had traveled from an area near Gambia in West Africa, was docked there. Its human cargo was on the dock for all to see or buy.

According to the 1838 publication *Memoir and Poems of Phillis Wheatley, a Native African and a Slave*, Susanna Wheatley saw "several robust, healthy females" and could have bid on them, but her attention was caught by a slender, naked girl who was likely seven or eight since she was losing her baby teeth. Susanna was taken by the "humble and modest demeanor and the interesting features of the little stranger." As suggested by Vincent Carretta in *Phillis Wheatley: Biography of a Genius in Bondage*, perhaps the girl evoked thoughts for Susanna of her own daughter, Sarah, who was almost that same age when she died on May 11, 1752. She chose the girl and named her Phillis Wheatley—Phillis for the ship, and Wheatley to match her own last name.

Phillis Wheatley.
Library of Congress LC-USZC4 5316

Phillis was frail. Perhaps it was the result of conditions on the nearly eight-month voyage she made with the 75 other enslaved Africans—men, women, and children. Given her age and gender, Phillis would have been allowed to spend much of her time on deck to breathe fresh air because she posed no threat, while the rest of the time she and the others would have been in the dark hold of the ship, below deck, without sanitary facilities. Most likely she saw some of the men chained to the bottom or sides of the hold. When she went to sleep, she would have leaned on one of the other women, many would have been ill from the voyage. Had she died, she would have been tossed overboard.

Susanna Wheatley's intention that day at the Beach Street wharf had been to select a young house servant. Her slaves were getting older and she, at age 52, was aging as well. Susanna introduced Phillis to her 18-year-old twin children, Mary and Nathaniel. In the weeks and months that followed, the family heard Phillis saying words in English. They saw her trying to write out individual letters—*a* or *b* or *c*—imitating what she saw Susanna or Mary or the others doing. Mary soon became Phillis's tutor. Within a year and a half, Phillis was able to read complex passages from the Bible. She attended church at Old South Meeting House and later became a full member of that church.

Five years later, at age 12, Phillis was writing poems. Her first one was written to a minister of the Old South Meeting House. When she was 14 years old, her first published poem, "On Messrs. Hussey and Coffin," appeared in the *Newport Mercury* newspaper on December 21, 1767. She was also studying religion with Rev. Dr. Richard Sewell, a man whose family was well known for its antislavery beliefs. While Phillis was a slave, she wasn't living like most slaves but was more like a member of the Wheatley family. Susanna didn't ask her to do many household tasks and intentionally kept her isolated from the other slaves.

Phillis later wrote of the dramatic events of her life and of her religious beliefs in a poem: "On Being Brought from Africa to America."

'Twas mercy brought me from my Pagan land,
Taught my benighted soul to understand
That there's a God, that there's a Saviour too . . .
Once I redemption neither sought nor knew, . . .

Phillis also used her poems to comment on the events occurring in Boston leading up to the American Revolution. One was a poem to King George III, ruler of Britain: "Rule thou in peace, our father, and our lord."

Another poem, "On the Death of Mr. Snider Murder'd by Richardson," criticized British actions in 1770 when 11-year-old Christopher Snider was killed when customs informer Ebenezer Richardson fired into a crowd: "With unexpected infamy disgraced / Be Richardson for ever banish'd here."

When Phillis was 16 or perhaps 17, she wrote a poem on the death of Boston evangelist George Whitefield that brought attention to her talent as a poet. The notice prompted Susanna to take action to have Phillis's poems published in a book. A prospective publisher, however, had some doubts, wondering if Phillis actually wrote the poems herself, without any help.

Again Susanna stepped in. She arranged for 18 prominent Bostonians to attest to her talent. The men included Governor Thomas Hutchinson, Lieutenant Governor Andrew Oliver, John Hancock, president of the Second Continental Congress and later a signer of the Declaration of Independence, and 15 others, most of whom were already familiar with her poems. The men agreed that, yes, Phillis was capable, and they believed her to be the author of her poems.

Susanna wanted to see Phillis's poems in print and took the next step. She knew that if a book—any book—was dedicated to a person of importance, it could help with the book's success. She asked Selina Hastings, the Countess of Huntingdon if Phillis could dedicate the book to her. Selina, impressed with Phillis's poems, agreed and also agreed to become her patron and requested an engraving be done of Phillis for the book. It was presumed to have been done by enslaved African American artist Scipio Moorhead.

Susanna also placed ads in Boston newspapers telling of Phillis's talent and of the upcoming book. Phillis, however, was ill, suffering from asthma, and the Wheatley's family doctor thought an ocean voyage might improve her poor health. Since Susanna's son, Nathaniel, was about to sail for London on family business, Susanna decided to send Phillis along on the voyage. It would give Phillis the opportunity to meet Selina Hastings and to be in London for the publication of her book. The *Massachusetts Gazette* and the *Boston Weekly News-Letter* of May 13, 1773, included the announcement:

> Boston, May 10, 1773 Saturday last Capt. Calef sailed for London, in [with] whom went Passengers Mr. Nathaniel Wheatley, Merchant; also, Phillis, the extraordinary Negro Poet, Servant to Mr. John Wheatley.

In turn, the 20-year-old Phillis expressed her emotions about her failing health and Susanna's sadness about the upcoming trip in "Farewell to America," a poem she dedicated to Mrs. Susanna Wheatley.

> *I mourn for Health deny'd . . .*
> *Susannah mourns, nor can I bear*
> *To see the Christal Show'r*
> *Fast Falling—the indulgent Tear*
> *In sad Departure's Hour.*

When Phillis arrived in London, she was well received. She met with Benjamin Franklin, one of the signers of the Declaration of Independence and Granville Sharp, a leader in the struggle to end slavery in Britain. She was set to meet with King George III and with Selina Hastings, her patron. She surely was looking forward to seeing her book in print, to looking at the words on the title page: *Poems on Various Subjects, Religious and Moral by Phillis Wheatley.* It would be the first book published by an African American woman and only the second book published by an American woman.

Then Phillis received news that Susanna Wheatley was ill and wanted her to return immediately to Boston. Surely disappointed but concerned, Phillis boarded a ship that set sail for America.

In the meantime, when her book came out in London, it was an immediate success and was used as proof of the intellectual ability of Africans, an issue debated at the time.

Yet, despite the acclaim, Phillis was still a slave. Soon after the book's publication and her return to America, the Wheatleys granted Phillis her freedom, though she continued to live with the family. She cared for the ailing Susanna for the next three months until she died on March 3, 1774, at the age of 65. In a letter to a friend, Phillis wrote:

> Let us imagine the loss of a parent, sister or brother. The tenderness of these was united in her. I was a poor little outcast and stranger when she took me in; not only into her house, but I presently became a sharer in her most tender affections. I was treated by her more like her child than her servant.

Two months later, after Phillis's return to Massachusetts in November 1773, 300 copies of her book arrived in America. All copies quickly sold. In June of the following year, the British blockaded the Boston Harbor and only one more shipment of her books arrived, somehow getting through the blockade. With the success of Phillis's book, she became the most renowned black person in the colonies.

As Phillis, now a free woman, worked to generate income for herself by continuing to write poems, regiments of British troops landed in Boston and marched the streets. Ships of war arrived in port. And Phillis Wheatley, on October 26, 1775, then in Rhode Island, wrote a letter to George Washington, enclosing a poem that acknowledged the importance of his position. It ended with the lines:

> *Proceed, great chief, with virtue on thy side,*
> *Thy every action let the goddess glide.*
> *A crown, a mansion, and a throne that shine,*
> *With gold unfading, WASHINGTON! be thine.*

When Washington received Phillis's letter, he first put it aside, then later passed it on to his former military aide, Joseph Reed, on February 10, 1776, along with a note:

> I recollect nothing else worth giving you the trouble of, unless you can be amused by reading a letter and poem addressed to me by Miss Phillis Wheatley. In searching over a parcel of papers the other day, in order to destroy such as were useless, I brought it to light again. At first, with a view of doing justice to her poetical genius, I had a great mind to publish the poem; but not knowing whether it might be considered rather as

a mark of my own vanity, than a compliment to her, I laid it aside, till I came across it again in the manner just mentioned.

A few days later, Washington wrote to Phillis:

Cambridge, Mass.
February 28, 1776

Miss Phillis, Your favor of the 26th of October did not reach my hands, till the middle of December. Time enough, you will say, to have given an answer ere this. Granted. But a variety of important occurances, continually interposing to distract the mind and withdraw the attention, I hope will apologize for the delay, and plead my excuse for the seeming but not real neglect. I thank you most sincerely for your polite notice of me, in the elegant lines you enclosed; and however undeserving I may be of such encomium and panegyric, the style and manner exhibits a striking proof of your poetical talents; in honor of which, and as a tribute justly due to you, I would have published the poem, had I not been apprehensive, that, while I only meant to give the world this new instance of your genius, I might have incurred the imputation of vanity. This, and nothing else, determined me not to give it place in the public prints.

If you should ever come to Cambridge, or near headquarters, I shall be happy to see a person so favored by the Muses, and to whom nature has been so liberal and beneficent in her dispensations. I am, with great respect, Your obedient humble servant,

GEORGE WASHINGTON.

That could have been the end of it: a private letter between one person and another. But Joseph Reed picked up the hint given him by Washington. He sent the poem and letter to the editors of the *Virginia Gazette*, and they were published on March 20, 1776. Thomas Paine, author of *Common Sense*, a document that inspired American patriots in 1776 to declare independence from Britain, republished the letter and poem in the April 1776 issue of a magazine called the *Pennsylvania Magazine: or, American Monthly Museum*.

As Phillis's voice heralded Washington and the Revolution, her own life changed drastically. John Wheatley died at age 72, in 1778, and left her nothing in his will. Mary died soon after, and her brother, Nathaniel, had moved to London and died in 1783. She was on her own, without the support of family.

In 1778 Phillis married a freedman, John Peters, a grocer, and she continued to speak out in poetry. In one of the poems, "Liberty and Peace," which she wrote under the name Phillis Peters, she wrote of the Peace of Paris, the set of treaties that ended the American Revolution. It ended with the lines:

Let virtue reign and thou accord our prayers,
Be victory ours and generous freedom theirs.

Phillis and her new husband had both been freed. Years earlier, in 1774, she had sent her thoughts on slavery in a letter to the Reverend Samson Occom. She wrote, "God has implanted a Principle which we call freedom; it is impatient of Oppression, and pants for Deliverance."

Unfortunately, her new life came with challenges and heartbreak. Her husband, while initially prosperous, had financial problems due to the harsh economic situation after the war—which was especially difficult for freed African Americans—and was often in debt. Eventually Phillis and John lived in poverty. Phillis cleaned houses to help support them and persisted unsuccessfully in her efforts to find a publisher for her second volume of poems, which was never published and has not survived. While John and Phillis were reported to have had three children who died while very young, "no birth, baptismal, or burial records have been found for any of the children of Phillis and John Peters." While John was imprisoned for debt in 1784, Phillis died at the age of 31, on December 5, probably as a result of chronic asthma.

Phillis Wheatley used her pen as her means of action in revolutionary America. She wrote of and for America, and her thoughts expressed in her poems still matter. Her voice is still heard.

LEARN MORE

Phillis Wheatley: Biography of a Genius in Bondage by Vincent Carretta (University of Georgia Press, 2011)

Phillis Wheatley Complete Writings by Phillis Wheatley (Penguin Books, 2001)

The Trial of Phillis Wheatley
www.thetrialofphilliswheatley.net

Mary Katherine Goddard

◆◆◆

A PATRIOTIC PUBLISHER

Mary Katherine Goddard spread the news of the event that sparked the American Revolution.

> Baltimore: April 26. We have just received the following important Intelligence. . . . Be it known that this morning, before Break of Day, a Brigade, consisting of about 1000 or 1200 men, landed at Phip's Farm, at Cambridge, and marched to Lexington, where they found a Company of our Colony Militia in Arms, upon whom they fired, without any Provocation, and killed 6 men, and wounded 4 others. . . . Printed by Mary K. Goddard.

Mary Katherine was the publisher of Baltimore's *Maryland Journal*, the first and only newspaper in that city. Her brother, William, had started the paper and was the owner. News of every sort filled the *Maryland Journal*:

Mary Katherine Goddard.
*Courtesy of the John Carter Brown
Library at Brown University*

Able-bodied free-
men from the ages
of 17 to 50 could
enlist for a three
year period. Bounties
of twenty dollars and a
suit of clothes were used
to attrack recruits . . .

Mrs. Smith, in the 109th year of her age, who lately
danced at a wedding, and sung a song of thirteen verses
distinctly . . . she mounts horse with great ability . . .

SIXTY DOLLARS Reward
    Ran away from the subscriber, living near Annapolis,
the 20th of May last, a Mulatto Slave named PETER,
a likely well made fellow, about 5 feet 8 inches high,
and 23 years of age . . . a great rogue.

At the time of the American Revolution, news was printed
on broadsides—long, single sheets of paper, almost like post-
ers. People read broadsides of papers like the *Maryland Journal*
to find out what was happening in that time before radio, TV,

telephones, Twitter, or the Internet. Announcements of plays
and church sermons printed on broadsides were distributed to
subscribers. The *Maryland Journal* also featured ads.

George Washington of Mt. Vernon in Virginia offers
for sale twenty thousand acres of western lands.

Thirty Dollars Reward
Strayed or stolen from Baltimore-Town . . . white
HORSE . . . he paces, trots, and canters; he has lost
one of his eyes . . .

Wants A Place
A MAN and his WIFE, who are capable of taking
charge of a plantation. The Man understands accounts.
. . . The Woman is well acquainted with the manage-
ment of *a dairy.*

The lives of Mary Katherine and her brother, William,
were intertwined from birth. They were the children of Giles

Masthead of the *Maryland Journal.*
Library of Congress; photo by Susan Casey

TO BE SOLD,

THE good SCHOONER SUCCESS, with all her materials as she came from sea, now lying at Chincoteague, burthen seventy tons, a remarkable fast sailing vessel, and well found. For terms, apply to WILLIAM NEIL, Baltimore, or the Captain on board.

Baltimore, Aug. 5, 1777.

An ad for a schooner for sale that appeared in the *Maryland Journal*, August 12, 1777. *Library of Congress; photo by Susan Casey*

Sterling,

THE *property of Harry Dorsey Gough, Esq; stands at the subscriber's plantation,* 6 *miles from Baltimore, where he will cover at Three Pounds the season.* He *is a beautiful black,* 7 *years old this Spring, upwards of* 15 *hands and a half high, well made in proportion, and is allowed, by the best judges, to be the handsomest Horse in this State ;* he *was got by Col. Sharpe's noted old Othello, out of a remarkable fine imported Dray Mare, and is what is called the Coach Horse. From this strain, out of light Mares, they breed those noble horses called Hunters, preferred to any in the world for the saddle or carriage.*

JAMES GOVANE.

March 22, 1777.

An ad for a horse for sale, *Maryland Journal*, April 15, 1777. *Library of Congress; photo by Susan Casey*

Goddard, a physician and a postmaster in New London, Connecticut, and Sarah Updike, a highly educated woman whose ancestors were among the first settlers of Rhode Island. Sarah tutored the siblings in French, Latin, and the classics.

When William left home to be a printer's apprentice on a newspaper, New Haven's *Connecticut Gazette*, it was the start of a series of newspaper ventures that soon involved both Mary Katherine and her mother. After Giles Goddard died, Sarah lent her son the money to set up a printing business in Providence, Rhode Island. When he needed help, Sarah and Mary Katherine joined him at the paper he started there, the *Providence Gazette*, and the women learned the printing trade. The mother-daughter team took over when William left to work on and start other papers, and the pair published the *Providence Gazette* from late 1765 to November 1768. Other women in other colonies were also running newspapers.

Sarah and Mary Katherine not only published the newspaper, but also wrote and edited the stories, sold subscriptions, and collected the debts when subscribers didn't pay. The entrepreneurial pair also printed almanacs, pamphlets, and books, and they opened a bookstore and bindery.

To print pages of the *Providence Gazette*, Sarah and Mary Katherine put on large aprons, rolled up the sleeves of their dresses, and set the type using printer's sticks to hold together small pieces of metal that were topped with raised letters that formed words, lines, and paragraphs. The women, like other printers, used leather balls to spread ink on the metal letters. After putting paper over the inked letters, they used a hand press to transfer the ink off the metal onto the paper. They pulled the paper off then let it dry.

Mary Katherine and Sarah might well have continued to publish the *Providence Gazette*, but William asked them to move to Philadelphia and assist him on a paper he started there, the *Philadelphia Chronicle and Universal Advertiser.* His mother protested, not wanting to move to a new place at her age of almost 70. But in 1768, both Sarah and Mary Katherine joined him. Sarah died two years later in 1770.

William and Mary Katherine worked on the *Philadelphia Chronicle and Universal Advertiser* until May 1773, when William moved to Baltimore to start yet another paper, the *Maryland Journal.* Mary Katherine successfully ran the Philadelphia paper herself but left it when William appealed to her to take over the *Maryland Journal.*

On February 17, 1774, Mary Katherine informed readers of the *Maryland Journal* that she would conduct the newspaper and printing business of her brother while he was away establishing a postal system to replace the British one. It was later adopted by the Continental Congress and is today the United States Postal Service. Through the influence of her brother, Mary Katherine then became the postmaster of Baltimore in addition to being the publisher of the *Maryland Journal.*

The *Maryland Journal* thrived under her leadership. It was read not only in Maryland but also in other colonies at a time when many other journals had gone out of business. That was no small feat for Mary Katherine. When there was a paper shortage during the Revolution, she managed by printing broadsides on small-sized sheets of paper. When subscribers couldn't pay, she accepted beef, beeswax, and other foods as payment. To supplement her income, she also ran a book bindery.

Almost a year after taking over the paper, in the issue dated May 10, 1775, Mary Katherine acknowledged her role on the paper to its readers by printing at the bottom of the broadside: "published by M. K. Goddard." It was only a month after the battle at Lexington and Concord.

Then she took an even bolder step. The first broadside featuring the Declaration of Independence had been printed and distributed by John Dunlap of Philadelphia. The Continental Congress, the ruling body of the colonies, was in Philadelphia and had commissioned it. That printing of the Declaration of Independence didn't include the names of the signers other than John Hancock and Charles Thompson. Why? The signers were considered traitors by the British and were fearful of British responses. Emotions ran high, and there were some real consequences. For example, when British troops arrived on Long Island in September 1776, they set out to find one of the signers, Francis Lewis, and when they couldn't find him, they wrecked his home and made his wife, Elizabeth Lewis, a prisoner.

As the war continued and after the British took over Philadelphia, the Continental Congress set up in Baltimore, Maryland, home of the *Maryland Journal*. Stories in the paper told of the Congress's arrival and of events of the war that didn't favor the revolutionary cause. Then at the end of the year, after wins at Trenton and Princeton, New Jersey, the members of the Continental Congress were encouraged. Perhaps the Revolution would be a success. They wanted to reaffirm their stance and ordered a printing of the Declaration of Independence that included the names of all the signers. They turned to Mary Katherine Goddard to publish it in the *Maryland Journal*.

Mary Katherine didn't merely print the document on the front page on January 18, 1777, she also applauded it. On the bottom of the document, instead of the usual, "Printed by M. K. Goddard," she included her full name—"Printed by Mary Katharine Goddard"—boldly acknowledging her personal support for the revolutionary cause. And she included a comment in the paper: "This was by no means the first printing of the Declaration of Independence for there had been at least eight before it,

but it was the first official issue with the names of the signers."
(Note: She spelled her name differently on the Declaration than
she did normally. At the time people could sometimes spell their
names different ways at different times.)

Thirteen years later, in 1789, the year that the US Constitu-
tion was adopted, Mary Katherine gave up her position as publisher of the *Maryland Journal* after a dispute with her brother.
She also lost her position as postmaster. New administrators
informed her that in the future the job would entail more traveling throughout the southern states than could be expected of
a woman. She didn't agree. She fought to retain her position by
appealing to George Washington and Congress. More than 200
Baltimore businessmen enthusiastically endorsed her petition,
wary of losing her for someone who might not have been as
proficient, to no avail.

Mary Katherine persevered. She retained a printing business
and in addition opened a bookstore and ran it until 1802. She
died in Baltimore on August 12, 1816. In her will, she freed her
slave, Belinda Starlin, and left all of her property to Belinda.

What is her legacy? Mary Katherine Goddard embraced a
profession dominated by men and held her own. She succeeded
as a newspaperwoman, postmaster, and store owner. And she
proclaimed her support for the American Revolution in print.
Mary Katherine Goddard deserves a high rank among women
of the Revolutionary War.

Early American Women Printers and Publishers, 1639–1820 by Leona Hudak (Scarecrow Press, 1978)

"Mary Katherine Goddard"
Women in the U.S. Postal System
Smithsonian National Postal Museum
http://postalmuseum.si.edu/WomenHistory/women_history
/history_goddard.html

"Mary Katherine Goddard (1738–1816)"
Maryland State Archives
http://msa.maryland.gov/megafile/msa/speccol/sc3500
/sc3520/002800/002809/html/2809bio.html

"Mary Katherine Goddard (1738–1816)"
National Women's History Museum
www.nwhm.org/education-resources/biography/biographies
/mary-katherine-goddard

Elizabeth Hutchinson Jackson

MOTHER TO THE END

In the spring of 1765, Elizabeth Hutchinson Jackson's "snapping blue eyes" were wide open and her red hair was surely blowing in the breeze on the ocean journey. She and her husband, Andrew, and their two sons—Hugh, two, and Robert, five months—had left Ireland and were on their way to America. Four of Elizabeth's sisters had moved there before them and written letters telling them of the opportunity to own land there, something the couple could probably never do in Ireland.

After the family arrived in Charleston, South Carolina, they mounted horses and joined the many other immigrants traveling south on the Catawba Path, then rode in a wagon on the dirt road that led to the backcountry of the Carolinas to the area called the Waxhaws, where Elizabeth's sisters welcomed them.

Elizabeth and Andrew claimed 200 acres near her sisters' homes. With the help of family and neighbors, they built a simple cabin, moved in, and called it home. Life was busy. While Andrew cleared the forest to create farmland, Elizabeth milked the cows, tended the garden, spent time on her spinning wheel, prepared meals, and cared for the boys.

Two years later, Andrew harvested their first crop. This was most likely a cause for celebration. But not long after, Elizabeth's life changed when Andrew unexpectedly died while working their land.

After his burial, Elizabeth, who was pregnant with their third child, and the boys stayed at the home of one of her sisters. Three days later, on March 15, 1767, without her husband to share the experience, Elizabeth gave birth to their third son and named the baby Andrew for his father.

Since it would have been difficult for Elizabeth to have handled the responsibilities of the home and farm by herself, she and her three boys moved into the home of her sister Jane Crawford. Jane also needed the help since she wasn't well. Elizabeth agreed to care for her and run the household for Jane's husband and their four sons and continued when Jane died not long after.

Life wasn't all work. Neighbors in the Waxhaws took breaks from their daily chores to visit with their neighbors. For example, they gathered in August 1776 to listen to the reading of the Philadelphia newspapers when they arrived a month or so after publication. The news in the papers that day was of the events of July 4, 1776. Elizabeth likely was proud when nine-year-old Andrew was selected as the reader. On that day, he read: "In Congress, July 4, 1776, the Unanimous Declaration of the Thirteen United States of America." Surely no one at the gathering suspected the significance of the nine-year-old Andrew reading the Declaration of Independence. He was to later become the seventh President of the United States of America—Andrew Jackson.

At the time, though, no one knew his future or if the new nation would succeed. The focus of the war between Britain and the colonies had shifted to the South, to the Carolinas. Elizabeth surely wondered how it would affect her family and soon found out. Her oldest son, Hugh, 16, joined the militia company of his uncle, Captain Robert Crawford. Even though he was ill and ordered not to fight, Hugh took part in the action at Stono Ferry, a battle fought on June 20, 1779, near Charleston, South Carolina. The day was excessively hot. Exhausted by the heat and fatigue, Hugh died after the battle, one of 34 Americans who died in that conflict.

That would have been a blow to any mother. Almost a year later, in an extremely bloody clash on May 29, 1780, between the British and the American patriots in the Jacksons' neighborhood in the Waxhaws, 113 patriot soldiers were killed and 150 wounded. Elizabeth took her other sons, Robert and Andrew, with her to the Waxhaw Church, and the three cared for the many wounded soldiers lying on the church floor.

The fighting had been fierce. Elizabeth, whose nickname was Betty, decided to take Robert and Andrew with some of the Crawfords to nearby North Carolina, where they would be safer.

Yet after a short time, Elizabeth, Robert, and Andrew returned to the Waxhaws. The situation had intensified. Men and boys were not leaving to fight in battles but fighting in their own neighborhoods to protect their homes against assaults by British troops or Tories. Elizabeth couldn't keep Robert, 16, and Andrew, 13, from joining in the defense. They rode their own horses and carried their own rifles and swords for protection. Andrew Jackson later wrote, "I was well fitted, being a good rider and knowing all the roads."

One night, fearful of being caught by British dragoons they'd spied the night before, Robert and Andrew slept in the woods; then, in the morning, they cautiously made their way home.

They got home safely, but as they were eating breakfast they heard horses approaching. The boys tried to hide while Elizabeth went to the door, but the British soldiers rushed in, challenging the family. When a British officer ordered Andrew to clean his boots, Andrew refused. The officer, thinking him to be impertinent, raised his sword and attempted to bring it down on Andrew's head. In defense, Andrew put up his arm to block the blow and suffered cuts not only to his scalp but also to his hand while other British soldiers pushed Betty aside.

Robert was also hit, and his head wounds were deeper. If the boys had been allowed to stay at home, their wounds would most likely have quickly healed. Instead, their wounds festered as the British took the brothers prisoner and forced them and other Waxhaw boys to walk 40 miles to be imprisoned at

The Currier & Ives depiction of Elizabeth Jackson being pushed aside as her son, Andrew Jackson, who would become the seventh President of the United States, is threatened and wounded by a British soldier.
Library of Congress LC-USZ62-2340

Camden. On the way, the brothers had to wade through creeks and keep up the pace without being allowed to stop to rest or drink water. When they arrived they were confined in a brick jail in Camden.

Elizabeth wanted her sons out of jail. After a short time had passed, she mounted a horse and rode 40 miles to the prison when she heard of the possibility of freeing her sons in an exchange. What was an exchange? If the British captured patriot soldiers, they imprisoned them, and the Americans did the same with British prisoners. If a soldier agreed not to continue to fight the enemy, he could be paroled or freed. Or soldiers of one army could be freed in exchange for soldiers of the other army being freed. In this case, Elizabeth became involved in an exchange that freed her sons and five Waxhaw neighbors.

When Robert and Andrew were released, Andrew was shoeless and without a coat. Robert, suffering from smallpox, was unable to hold himself on a horse. With Elizabeth on one horse, Robert tied onto another, and Andrew walking alongside, the three made their way home. As Andrew undoubtedly told his mother as they traveled, his shoes and coat had been taken while he was in jail, his wounds had worsened, and he had been given little food.

As they neared home on the last night of their journey, a fierce rainstorm pelted them. By the time they arrived, Robert was delirious, and in two days he was dead.

Elizabeth hardly had time to grieve for him before she saw red spots on Andrew's face and hands, signs that he too had contracted smallpox, the disease that had killed Robert. Elizabeth spent months nursing Andrew back to health. He also suffered from the chills and fever of malaria.

As Andrew healed, Elizabeth's thoughts turned to her nephews, William and Joseph (the sons of her sister Jane), whom she had helped raise. They had also been captured and were prisoners of war, confined on a prison ship. She wanted to do for them what their own mother, long dead, could not do: bring them home. Along with two other women, she planned again to mount her horse and head for a jail in hopes of an exchange.

Before she left, Elizabeth talked to Andrew about her values, ones she thought were important. According to *Young Hickory: The Making of Andrew Jackson*, she told him, "Make friends by being honest . . . keep them by being steadfast. Andrew, never tell a lie or take what is not yours. . . . Never sue for slander. Settle them cases yourself."

Elizabeth and her two friends mounted their horses for the three-to-four-day journey to Charleston, where her nephews were imprisoned. Once there, and while waiting for the exchange, she nursed other mothers' sons. Exposure to the diseases of the soldiers sickened her, and she died. When Elizabeth's two companions returned to the Waxhaws, they gave her few belongings to 14-year-old Andrew. He later wrote, "I felt utterly alone and tried to recall her last words to me."

With her example of persistence to follow, he made his way. He took up the study of law and eventually started a law practice in Tennessee. In 1829, at age 61, Andrew Jackson was sworn in as President of the United States of America.

Andrew Jackson later said, "The memory of my mother and her teachings were after all the only capital I had to start in life, and on that capital I have made my way."

LEARN MORE

Andrew Jackson: His Life and Times by H. W. Brands (Doubleday, 2005)

The Life of Andrew Jackson by Robert V. Remini (Harper & Row, 1988)

Young Hickory: The Making of Andrew Jackson by Hendrik Booraem (Taylor Trade Publishing, 2001)

Esther Reed and
Sarah Franklin Bache

SUPPORTERS OF THE TROOPS

Who dared to argue with George Washington, commander in chief of the Continental Army? Esther Reed. But she had the best of intentions: Esther wanted to help the ordinary soldiers.

Esther wasn't just anyone. Her husband, Joseph Reed, had become George Washington's military secretary in 1775, and later, as of 1778, he was president of the Supreme Executive Council of Pennsylvania, the equivalent of governor of Pennsylvania and a member of the Continental Congress. Esther, in turn, had a position of influence.

So how did Esther Reed come to argue with General Washington? Esther wanted to help the Continental Army soldiers in one way, and George Washington wanted to help them in a different way.

Esther de Berdt was born in England, the daughter of a successful trader. She was well educated, refined, and likely popular at the gatherings her father hosted at his home for the young men from America who were studying in London. She caught the eye of American law student Joseph Reed, and the two courted. Then, when Reed returned to America to deal with family business, they corresponded by letter for five years. When Reed returned to England, intending to marry Esther and take up residence in that city, he discovered that Esther's father had died during his absence. Plans changed. After the couple married in May 1770 at St. Luke's church in London, they moved to America and made their home in Philadelphia, Pennsylvania.

Esther Reed.
The Pictorial Field-Book of the Revolution *by Benson J. Lossing, 1860*

During the Revolutionary War, Joseph Reed kept his wife informed about the reality of war. In a 1778 letter to a friend, Esther wrote, "My dear Mr. Reed was in the action [at Monmouth], and had his horse again shot." She

Joseph Reed.
The Pictorial Field-Book of the Revolution *by Benson J. Lossing, 1860*

knew from him that the soldiers often didn't have enough to eat or blankets to protect them from the cold in winter, that their clothes were worn, that they had to sleep in places that were

Sarah Franklin Bache.
The Pictorial Field-Book of the Revolution *by Benson J. Lossing, 1860*

often damp and unsanitary, that diseases such as smallpox and typhus killed thousands of them and that many of them were not receiving their promised pay.

Esther decided to do something about the situation and took the bold step of publishing a broadside in June 1780 titled, "The Sentiments of an American Woman." She included the lines, "If I live happy in the midst of my family . . . it is to you [the soldiers] that we owe it. And shall we hesitate to evidence to you our gratitude?" Her essay was an appeal to the most prominent women of her city, wives of leading patriot leaders, to act together to support the fighting men. It was a call for them to do more than cheer on the soldiers.

Sarah Franklin Bache, whose father, Benjamin Franklin, was one of the Founding Fathers, ambassador to France, and an inventor, responded and influenced 35 other Philadelphia ladies to become involved as well. Only three days after the publication of the essay, the women met to form the Ladies Association of Philadelphia. Esther, elected president, and the other ladies decided to organize a fundraising effort so they could "render the condition of the soldier more pleasant."

The Ladies Association of Philadelphia demonstrated their organizational skills by dividing the city of Philadelphia into 10 areas, then assigning pairs of women to canvass each area. In doing so, they stepped out of the normal patterns of their lives. "They normally would not have engaged in such public displays of political activities but then these were hardly normal circumstances. All sort of things were turned upside down and the project was an ideal opportunity for women to demonstrate their skills, their power, their patriotism," says Vivian Bruce Conger, Historian, Ithaca College.

Picture them traveling in pairs, knocking on each door. They asked anyone who answered to donate to the cause of the Revolution. They even knocked on the doors of those who were pro-British! One of those loyalist ladies, 23-year-old Anna Rawle Clifford, didn't think too highly of them. She wrote, "People were obliged to give them something to get rid of them." And Anna noted that the ladies didn't just ask other women:

> The gentlemen were also honored with their visits. Bob Wharton declares he was never so teased in his life. They reminded him of the extreme rudeness of refusing anything to the fair sex; but he was inexorable and pleaded want of money, and the heavy taxes, so at length they left him, threatening to hand his name down to posterity with infamy.

In all, Esther, Sarah, and the others secured 1,645 contributions, more than $300,000 in Continental Dollars, or $7,500 in coin and gold. According to *Life and Correspondence of Joseph Reed*, "All ranks of society seem to have joined in the liberal effort, from Phillis, the coloured woman with her humble seven shillings six pence, to the Marchioness de La Fayette, who contributed $100 in coin, and the Countess de Luzerne, who gave $6,000 in Continental paper."

Since Esther had sent notice of the campaign to adjoining counties and states, it wasn't just the women of Philadelphia who chipped in, but ladies from many different locations. Each area had its own treasures and all the collected funds were ultimately sent to Martha Washington who also participated in the campaign.

On July 4, 1780, Esther wrote to General Washington telling him of the results of their efforts and asking his opinion about how best to spend the money. She wrote: "The ladies are anxious for the soldiers to receive the benefit of it," she wrote, "and wait your directions how it can best be disposed of."

Washington wrote back on July 14, 1780, with his suggestion:

> If I am in having the concurrence of the Ladies, I would propose the purchasing of course Linnen, to be made into Shirts. . . . A Shirt extraordinary to the Soldier will be of more service, and do more to preserve his health than any other thing that could be procured him . . . provided it is approved of by the Ladies.

Esther and the other ladies, though, didn't want to use the money to buy shirts. Esther had heard that 2,000 shirts had been sent by the state of Pennsylvania to their soldiers and some had been brought by the French fleet, the new allies of the American forces. The Ladies Association of Philadelphia wanted to provide a different token of appreciation to the soldiers.

In a letter of July 31, 1780, she wrote to Washington again:

> An idea prevails among the ladies that the soldiers will not be so much gratified, by bestowing an article [a shirt] to which they are entitled from the public . . . propose the whole of the money be changed into hard dollars, find giving each solder two, to be entirely at his disposal . . .

The ladies wanted to give the soldiers money directly—two dollars each to spend as they wished. Two dollars doesn't sound like much today, but back then, it was a generous gift.

Washington wrote back on August 10, 1780, clearly expressing a different opinion:

> A taste of hard money may be productive of much discontent . . . a few provident soldiers will probably avail themselves of the advantages . . . but it is equally probable that it will be the means of bringing punishment on a number of others whose propensity to drinking . . . too frequently leads them into . . . disorder that must be corrected. A shirt would render the condition of the soldiery much more comfortable than it is at present.

It was a convincing argument. Esther and the others of the Ladies Association of Philadelphia knew that the new American government was unable to levy taxes and realized it couldn't afford to provide enough of the needed clothing. The women also decided to stretch the funds and increase the amount of their gift by making the shirts themselves. Esther wrote to Washington on August 10, 1780, that the ladies "had not the most distant wish that their donation should be bestowed in any manner, that did not perfectly accord with your opinion. I shall, without delay, put the plan into execution."

Esther shared the decision with her husband in a letter she wrote on August 22, 1780: "I shall now endeavor to get the shirts made as soon as possible."

As the women of the Ladies Association of Philadelphia bought the linen and began the shirt-making project, intertwining their efforts with the everyday activities of their lives, Esther did the same. In the same letter of August 22, Esther wrote to

Joseph that she was spending time outside the city with their five children, one only four months old and the other four younger than nine:

> Our dear little children are pretty well. Dennis has been most terribly bit with mosquitoes, which he scratched till they are very sore and trouble some, and it makes him fretful. The chief reason to make me regret leaving this place is on the children's account, who seem to enjoy more pleasure here than in town. . . .
>
> Adieu, my dear friend; think of me often, and remember with what sincere and tender affection I am unalterably and truly yours,
>
> E Reed.

It was a sweet good-bye. Then, only weeks later, Esther was stricken by a bout of dysentery and, without the strength to fight back, Esther died on September 18, 1780, at age 34. Her husband mourned her early death. On her tomb he had engraved:

> *In memory of Esther*
> *Venerate the ashes here entombed*
> *Think how slender is that thread on which the joys*
> *And hopes of life depend.*

After Esther's death, the Ladies Association of Philadelphia regrouped. Sarah Franklin Bache, born in 1743 and known as Sally by her friends, took over the leadership of the shirt project. Like Esther, she was well suited for the task. She had watched her mother, Deborah Read Franklin, run the family businesses (a book and stationery shop and a printing business) while her father, Benjamin Franklin, was away for long periods of time.

Sarah was educated by local schoolmasters in reading, writing, French, needlework, dancing, and music. She had many friends and attended balls in Philadelphia before the war and before her marriage to Richard Bache, a businessman. Sarah's father wasn't initially keen on the match because he didn't have confidence in Richard's ability to support his daughter. Her father's decision so upset Sarah that her mother sided with her, agreed to the marriage, and the couple married without Benjamin Franklin's consent. Franklin softened, however, after the birth of Sarah and Richard's first child, who was named after him, and after Bache experienced some success in business. The marriage was a happy one, and seven of the couple's eight children lived to be adults.

After Sarah's mother died in 1774, and when Benjamin Franklin was in Philadelphia, Sarah acted as her father's hostess, welcoming and entertaining her father's friends and political associates at the Franklin home. Perhaps she also performed; she was a skilled harpsichordist.

While Benjamin Franklin was clearly political, Sarah's involvement in the shirt project was a political act as well—an indication of her personal dedication to the Revolutionary cause. She shared the duties of the Ladies Association of Philadelphia with four other women—Mrs. Francis, Mrs. Hillegas, Mrs. Clarkson, and Mrs. Blair—and made her home the shirt-making workshop. Imagine the ladies spreading the linen on tables, using patterns, then cutting the linen, then chatting as they sewed the shirts. Sarah wrote to her father, "I have been busily employed in cutting out shirts and making them, and getting them made for our brave soldiers."

When the 2,005 shirts were finished, Sarah wrote to Washington:

> We packed up the shirts in three boxes, and delivered them to Colonel Miles, with a request that he would send them to Trenton immediately, lest the river should close, where they now wait your Excellency's orders. There are two thousand and five in number. They would have been at Camp long before this had not the general sickness prevented. We wish them to be worn with as much pleasure as they were made.

As more than 2,000 soldiers received the shirts, they were surely moved by the personal touch. Each woman—married and unmarried—had embroidered her name on each shirt she had made, making each a personal gift from one of the ladies of Philadelphia. It was also an expression of their patriotism. They could be wives, daughters, and mothers, and they could also be active patriots.

Washington was pleased with the results and wrote a note of thanks, including the comment, "The army ought not to regret their sacrifices or sufferings, when they meet with so flattering a reward as the sympathy of your sex."

Esther surely wouldn't have dared argue with that remark. Her voice was heard, as were the voices of Sarah Franklin Bache and the other powerful, brave women of the Ladies Association of Philadelphia.

George Washington's personal letter to Sarah Franklin Bache and the other Philadelphia women who organized the fundraising and shirt-making efforts attests to his admiration and appreciation of their efforts.

———————•———————

TO MRS. FRANCIS, MRS. HILLEGAS, MRS. CLARKSON, MRS. BACHE, AND MRS. BLAIR.
New Windsor, 13th February, 1781.

Ladies,

The benevolent office which added lustre to the qualities that ornamented your deceased friend, could not have descended to more zealous or more deserving successors. The contributions of the association you represent have exceeded what could have been expected, and the spirit that animated the members of it entitles them to an equal place with any who have preceded them on the walk of female patriotism. It embellishes the American character with a new trait, by proving that the love of country is blended with those softer domestic virtues which have always been allowed to be more peculiarly your own.

You have not acquired admiration in your own country only; it is paid to you abroad, and, you will learn with pleasure, by a part of your own sex whose female accomplishments have attained their highest perfection, and who, from the commencement, have been the patronesses of American liberty.

The army ought not to regret their sacrifices or sufferings, when they meet with so flattering a reward as the sympathy of your sex; nor can they fear that their interests will be neglected, while espoused by advocates as powerful as they are amiable. I can only answer to the sentiments, which you do me the honour to express for me personally, that they would more than repay a life devoted to the service of the public, and to testimonies of gratitude to yourselves. Accept the assurances of the perfect respect and esteem with which I am, ladies,

Your most obedient, &c.,

George Washington

LEARN MORE

American Women's History: An A-Z of People, Organizations, Issues, and Events by Doris L. Weatherford (Prentice Hall, 1994)

Founding Mothers: The Women Who Raised Our Nation by Cokie Roberts (HarperCollins Publishers Inc., 2004)

Patriots in Petticoats: Heroines of the American Revolution by Shirley Raye Redmond (Random House, 2004)

Revolutionary Mothers: Women in the Struggle for America's Independence by Carol Berkin (Alfred A. Knopf, 2005)

Women of the American Revolution (Vol. I), by Elizabeth F. Ellet, contains chapters on Esther Reed and Sarah Bache. http://archive.org or Google Books

Notable American Women 1607–1950, Volume I, Edited by Edward T. James, Janet Wilson, and Paul S Boyer (The Kelknap Press of Harvard University Press, 1971)

Elizabeth Burgin

THE RESCUER WHO BECAME A FUGITIVE

Sometimes only historical records relate the experiences of ordinary American women who lived during the Revolution. That is the case with Elizabeth Burgin. The few known details of her life are disclosed in letters written by her to the Reverend James Calville, to George Washington, and by Washington to others on her behalf.

In 1779 Elizabeth, a widow and mother, was suspected of helping American prisoners escape from British prisons. According to one of her letters, she was guilty. And on the run.

During the American Revolution, when the Americans won a battle, they would take the British soldiers prisoner, and vice versa. Neither side saw a reason to let enemy soldiers free to fight again. Around New York City alone, more than 11,000 colonists were taken prisoner by the British. Both the British and the Americans had to house prisoners wherever they could: jails, churches, halls, ships, or whatever space was at hand.

Conditions in the prisons were awful—overcrowded, unsanitary, with little in the way of food or care for prisoners, including those who were sick, wounded, or dying. One prisoner, a man named William Slade, wrote in his diary:

> Friday, 13th of December, 1776: A little water broth. We now see nothing but the mercy of God to intercede for us. Sorrowful times, all faces look pale, discouraged, discouraged.
>
> Tuesday, 17th of December, 1776. Suffer with cold and hunger. We are treated worse than cattle and hogs.
>
> Saturday, 21st of December, 1776. Last night one of our regiment got on shore, but got catched.
>
> Sunday, 22nd of December, 1776. Last night nothing but grones all night of sick and dying. . . . Death multiplies. . . . All faces sad.

On July 19, 1779, Elizabeth Burgin wrote of the consequences of her efforts to help American prisoners: "On July 17th I was sent

Interior view of a Revolutionary era prison, showing prisoners and guard.
Library of Congress, LC-USZ62-5852

for by General Pattison [the military commander of New York] suspected of helping American prisoners make their escape."

Along with a man named George Higday Elizabeth wrote that she "carried out Major van Burah and Captain Crain and Lieutenant Lee who made their escape from the guard on Long Island."

Who was George Higday and how does he figure into the story? Higday was either a spy or a potential one. British and Americans were using spies to gather information about what the other army was planning and doing. George Washington recruited one of his officers, Major Benjamin Tallmadge, to organize an intricate spy operation called the Culper Spy Ring. Washington wrote a letter to Tallmadge regarding a possible new recruit to the ring: George Higday, the man working with Elizabeth. Washington wrote:

Letter to Major Benjamin Tallmadge
New Windsor, 27 June, 1779

There is a man on York Island, living near the North River, by the name of George Higday who, I am told, has given signal proofs of his attachment to us, and at the same time stands well with the enemy. If, upon inquiry, this is found to be the case, he will be a fit instrument to convey intelligence to me while I am on the west side of the North River . . .

Unfortunately, that letter was intercepted by the British, who arrested Higday. Elizabeth's letter explained what happened as a result:

George Higday was taken up and confined. . . . His wife told General Pattison that he carried out 200 prisoners for me for which reason knowing myself guilty did hide myself for two weeks in New York understanding Gen Pattison had offered a bounty of two hundred pounds for taking me. He kept a guard for five days at my house letting nobody come in or out.

In other words, George Higday's wife pointed the finger at Elizabeth! Perhaps she thought that by implicating Elizabeth, her husband would be cleared or he might receive a lighter punishment. And what a reward! The £200 British bounty was the equivalent of 20 years of pay for a British soldier. Capturing Elizabeth and turning her in could have set a person up for life. Her letter continued:

Through the help of friends, I got on Long Island and there staid five weeks. Then, William Scudder came to Long Island in a whale boat and I made my escape with him. We [were] being chased by two boats halfway [across] the Sound . . . then got to New England and came to Philadelphia. Then I got a pass of the Board of War to go to Elizabeth Town to try to get my children from New York, which I obtained in three or four weeks, but could not get my clothes or anything but my children. When application was made by Mr. John Frankling, my close [clothes] and furniture, they should be sold and the money given to the loyler [lawyer].

In other words, Elizabeth was able to pick up her children, but all her possessions were to be sold and the money given to loyalists (those loyal to the British). It was a high price to pay for her brave efforts. Her letter continued with her plea for help:

I am now Sir, very desolate, without money, without cloaths [clothes] or friends to go to. I mean to go to Philadelphia, where God knows how I should live, a cold winter coming on. For the truth of the above your Excellency can inquire of Major John Stewart or Col Thomas Thomas. I lived opposite Mr. John Frankling and by their desire make this application, if your Excellency please you can direct to Mr. Thomas Frankling in Philadelphia where I can be found. If the general think proper I should be glad to draw provisions for myself and children in Philadelphia, where I mean to remain, helping our poor prisoners brought me to want, which I don't repent.

Elizabeth's letter was an impassioned plea for financial assistance from an ordinary woman. She had helped prisoners, was in a fix, and didn't repent her efforts. Her letter was ultimately directed to the Continental Congress. Many soldiers and wives appealed to the Continental Congress for financial help in exchange for their efforts during the Revolutionary War. Elizabeth's efforts came to the attention of George Washington. On Christmas Day in 1779, Washington wrote a letter to the Continental Congress on her behalf.

Head Quarters Morristown
25th December 1779.
Sir
I have the honor to lay before your Excellency the representation of a certain Elizabeth Burgin late an inhabitant of New-York. From the testimony of different persons, and particularly many of our own officers who have returned from captivity, it would appear that she

Letter of Elizabeth Burgin to Reverend James Calville. (The letter above as quoted in this chapter was edited for clarity.)
National Archives 5916026

has been indefatigable for the relief of the prisoners, and in measures for facilitating their escape. In consequence of this conduct she incurred the suspicions of the enemy and was finally compelled to make her escape, under the distressed circumstances which she describes. I could not forbear recommending to consideration a person who has risqued so much and been so friendly to our officers and privates, especially as to this we must attribute her present situation.

. . . I entertained of her services and sufferings have ventured to take the liberty of directing the commissary at Philadelphia to furnish her and her children with rations till the pleasure of Congress could be known. Congress will judge of its justice and propriety, and how much she may be entitled to further notice.

I have the honor to be with the greatest respect

Your Excellency's

Most Obt Servt

G Washington

George Washington attested to Elizabeth's efforts to aid the revolution after doing a bit of investigating on his own. He also arranged for her and her children to be provided with food rations, a compassionate act. Unfortunately, when the Continental Congress referred the matter to the Board of War, it was ignored.

Elizabeth needed a pension or a job. She wrote another letter "praying to be employed in cutting out linen for the use of the Army." It reached the Continental Congress which again referred her request to the Board of War. Finally, on August 10, 1781, the Board of War granted Elizabeth Burgin a pension of $53.50 per year, which she collected through 1787, presumably the year she died.

In one last letter to George Washington, Elizabeth wrote:

I received a kind letter from your aide-de-camp inform-ing me that your Excellency had recommended me to the honorable Continental Congress . . . thank you for all the favours I have received thus with my prayers for your welfare I conclude and make bold to subscribe myself your Excellency most obedient humble servant.

Signed Elizabeth Burgin

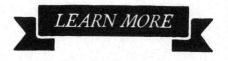

LEARN MORE

Forgotten Patriots: The Untold Story of American Prisoners during the Revolutionary War by Edwin G. Burrows (Basic Books, 2008)

George Washington letter to Benjamin Tallmadge, June 27, 1779
Collections of the Clements Library
http://clements.umich.edu/exhibits/online/spies/letter-1779jun27pub.html

Elizabeth Burgin Letter to Reverend James Calville, November 19, 1779
National Archives
http://research.archives.gov/description/5916026

George Washington letter to the President of Congress, December 25, 1779
National Archives
http://research.archives.gov/description/5913711

Elizabeth Burgin letter to George Washington,
March 16, 1780
National Archives
http://founders.archives.gov/documents/Washington/99-01
-02-01137

Part Two

SPIES

Lydia Darragh

◆◆◆

THE LISTENER WHO
ALERTED THE GENERAL

Light-haired, blue-eyed Lydia Darragh edged her way through the crowded streets of Philadelphia in 1777, jockeying for position with the 14,000 British troops occupying the American capital of Philadelphia, a city of 23,000. None of them likely suspected her of being a spy.

George Washington's Continental Army had been forced out of the city and was camped at Whitemarsh, 20 miles out of town. Philadelphia had been the capital of the new American nation, but the Continental Congress, the ruling body of the newly formed nation, had moved to Baltimore to avoid capture by the British.

Could Washington launch an attack, close off the city, trap the British, and regain the city? Maybe. Certainly he could benefit by knowing the plans of the British troops, and Lydia Darragh thought her son Charles, one of the soldiers camped at Whitemarsh, could help.

63

As she made her way through the city streets, perhaps to purchase flour from one of the mills on the outskirts of the city in order to make bread for her family, or to shop for meat or other things for her family, Lydia was surely alert to the conversations she overheard—comments like, "A number of troops have gone out of town," or, "There is talk today, as if a great part of ye English army were making ready to depart on some secret expedition."

After Lydia heard snippets like these, she told her husband, William, who had been the family tutor when she was growing up in Ireland. Lydia Barrington and William Darragh had married in Dublin, Ireland, on November 2, 1753, when she was 25 and he 34. They left Dublin behind, crossed the sea, and started their life together in Philadelphia. By 1777 they were the parents of five children.

William carefully wrote down in code the information Lydia shared with him, using symbols to represent words. When he finished, Lydia smoothed the paper, carefully molded it over a button, then covered the paper and button with fabric matching the coat of her 14-year-old son, John. After John put on the coat, he traveled to Whitemarsh, surely passing British soldiers on the way, until he reached the Continental Army camp and found his older brother, Charles.

Charles knew the routine, removed the fabric, translated the message from shorthand back into letters, and delivered the information to General Washington's headquarters.

Lydia Darragh's spy ring was quite a clever way of contributing to the war effort from a woman who, only 10 years prior, had posted an ad using her needle and thread skills in a very different way:

The Subscriber, living in Second street . . . takes this Method of informing the Public, that she intends to make Grave Clothes, and lay out the Dead, in the neatest Manner . . . she hopes, by her Care, to give Satisfaction to those who will be pleased to favour her with their Orders. Lydia Darragh.

During the years of 1777–1778 when the British Army occupied Philadelphia, British officers took over many of the homes in town, and those Philadelphia families had to find other places to live. General Sir William Howe, commander of the British Army, had taken over one house and made it his headquarters. The Darraghs lived in a building known as Loxley's House on South Second Street.

One day William Darragh answered a knock on the door. The soldier on the step informed him that the family must

Headquarters of British commander General Sir William Howe.
The Pictorial Field-Book of the Revolution *by Benson J. Lossing, 1860*

Loxley's House, the residence of the Darragh family.
The Pictorial Field-Book of the Revolution *by Benson J. Lossing, 1860*

find a new home because the British wanted to take over their house. When Lydia heard that news, she decided to visit British headquarters to speak with General Howe. As she waited, she began chatting with one of the British officers and discovered his last name was Barrington, the same as her maiden name. Soon Lydia and the officer discovered they were indeed from the same part of Ireland, and were second cousins!

Perhaps struck by the serendipity of their connection, the officer listened as Lydia told him of the difficulty of finding a home for her family in the already crowded city. He spoke to General Howe for her, and a compromise was reached. Lydia, William, and the children could stay in their home but had to give up a large room at the back of the house that British officers could use for meetings—a council room.

Officer Barrington and General Howe might have been swayed in Lydia's favor when discovering that the Darraghs were Quakers, a religious movement whose members declared themselves to be neutral in times of war. Of course, with a son in the army and with an active button-related spy system already in place, Lydia had broken with Quaker beliefs, but her reputation as a Quaker may have convinced the British military men to trust her.

Lydia and William took one action in response to the British setting up a council room in their house. They sent their two youngest children—William, 11, and Susannah, 9—to live with relatives outside of town.

In the days and weeks that followed, British officers came and went through the Darragh home, walking to and from the back room. An account published in 1827 by Lydia's daughter Ann, who was 21 at the time and residing with her mother, tells of the events that followed. (Ann's account was told to and recorded [on an unknown date] by Lydia's great-granddaughter, Margaret Porter Darragh, for the family history.)

According to Ann's account, the British officer who made arrangements for use of Lydia's back room told her "to have all her family in bed at an early hour, as they wished to use the room that night free from interruption."

That was on December 2, 1777. As Lydia lay in bed, thinking of that comment, she slipped out of bed and "into a closet, separated from the council room by a thin board partition covered with paper, just in time to hear the reading of the minutes of the council." She heard that the British troops were going to attack "Washington's army, and with their superior force and the unprepared condition of the enemy victory was certain. . . . A sharp pang shot through her heart."

According to Ann's account, Lydia then quickly returned to her bed and pretended she was fast asleep when the British officer knocked on her door once, twice, to let her know of their departure. On the third knock, she answered as if just having awoken. As he exited, Lydia put out the lights and locked the outside door.

The next day, according to Ann, Lydia spent her day thinking of what to do with the information. She didn't choose to relay it via buttons, but she did devise a plan. That night, she told William that she would use an old pass—Philadelphians needed passes in order to leave the city during the British occupation—to visit their younger children who lived outside the city. It's also said that she told William she was planning to go to a mill outside the city limits to buy flour.

Either way, she walked toward Whitemarsh by herself and, according to Ann, "did not tell her husband the real reason for her errand to the country until she thought the danger was over. . . . She feared the least suspicion of his having taken information out of the city might endanger his life."

On her way Lydia saw an American officer approaching on horseback. They recognized each other. Captain Craig of Washington's army "was greatly surprised to see her," Ann recounted, "and asked, 'Why, Mrs. Darragh, what are you doing so far from home?' She asks him to walk beside her, which he does, leading his horse. In low tones she tells him the important intelligence she has risked so much to bring, and he at once rides with it to headquarters."

Lydia probably didn't know that others were also passing on information about British plans to those in Washington's army. Bits of information about troop movements were trickling in from a variety of sources. Many people suspected something was about to happen. But when?

Captain Craig left Lydia, then made his way to the Rising Sun Tavern, where Colonel Elias Boudinot, who managed the intelligence for the Continental Army, was having dinner. Craig passed on the information to Boudinot. Yet Boudinot made a curious entry in his journal:

In Autumn of 1777 the American Army lay some time at White Marsh. I was then Commissary Genl of

Lydia Darragh passing secrets.
Pioneer Mothers of America *by Harry Clinton Green and Mary Wolcott Green, 1912*

Prisoners, and managed the Intelligence of the Army. I was reconoitering along the Lines near the City of Philadelphia. I dined at a small Post at the Rising Sun ab't three Miles from the City.

After Dinner, a little, poor looking, insignificant Old Woman came in & solicited leave to go into the Country to buy some Flour. While we were asking some questions, she walked up to me and put into my hands a dirty old Needle-Book, with various small Pockets in it—Surprised at this, I told her to retire—She should have our Answer—On opening the needlebook, I could not find anything, till I got to the last Pocket, where I found a piece of paper rolled up into the form of a Pipe shank—on unrolling it I found information that Genl Howe was coming out the next morning with 5,000 men, 13 pieces of cannon, baggage wagons, and 11 Boats on Waggon Wheels.

Was Lydia that old woman? Some say she was. Others suggest Lydia gave the information to another woman to deliver for her. According to one account, Colonel Craig took Lydia to a farmhouse along the road to rest and have something to eat and then, as suggested by Melissa Lukeman Bohrer in *Glory, Passion, and Principle*, Lydia could have given the information to a woman at the farmhouse who then passed it on to Boudinot.

Or perhaps Lydia delivered the information twice—once to Colonel Craig and then again to Boudinot—to make sure it got to Washington. Boudinot's account continued:

On comparing this with other information, I found it true and immediately rode Post to head Quarters— According to my usual Custom & agreeable to Orders

recd from Genl W. I first related to him the naked
Fact without comment or Opinion—He rec. it with
much thoughtfulness—I then gave him my opinion,
that General Howe's Design was to cross the Delaware
under Pretense of going to New York—Then in the
Night to recross the Delaware above Bristol & come
suddenly on our R, when we were totally unguarded.

Lydia returned to the mill that afternoon, picked up her bag
of flour, and returned home in early evening. When General
Howe and the British troops approached Washington's camp
the next day for a surprise attack, the Americans had their cannons mounted and troops ready. The British had to turn around
without attacking.

A victory for Washington! But for Lydia? Later that day, the
officer who had asked Lydia to have her family go to bed early
only two nights before knocked on her door and, according to
Ann Darragh's account,

called her to the council room and then locked the
door. She was so faint she would have fallen if he had
not handed her a chair and asked her to be seated. The
room was nearly dark, and he could not see the pallor
of her face. Then he inquired if any of her family were
awake on the night of their last council. She replied:
"No, they were all asleep." Then, he said: "I need not
ask you, for we had great difficulty in waking you to
fasten the door after us. But one thing is certain; the
enemy had notice of our coming, were prepared for us,
and we marched back like a parcel of damned fools. The
walls must have some ears."

Later, in relating the story to her friends and family, Lydia said, "I never told a lie about it. I could answer all his questions without that."

On December 10, six days later, George Washington wrote to the president of the Continental Congress, Henry Laurens: "In the course of the last week, from a variety of intelligence, I had reason to expect that General Howe was preparing to give us a general action."

WAS LYDIA'S STORY TRUE?

———— • ————

Due to the publication of Ann Darragh's account of her mother's activities as a spy, Lydia's story was celebrated by schoolchildren until 1877, when a man named Thompson Westcott challenged the story on a number of points. His arguments were included in the *American Quarterly Review* of 1827 and reprinted in the *Evening Bulletin* of 1909 along with the statement: "The story has been discredited." Westcott argued that Washington already knew of the impending attack, that Lydia didn't have time to walk there and back.

But in 1915 a man named Henry Darrach (no relation) countered Westcott's arguments in a publication by the City History Society of Philadelphia. The story of Lydia Darragh's delivery of information to George Washington continues to be doubted by some but believed by most.

Lydia and her family continued living in Loxley's House. In June 1778 the British left Philadelphia and moved to New York City. After the death of her husband on April 22, 1786, Lydia moved to another home in Philadelphia, where she lived and ran a store until she died on December 28, 1789, at the age of 61.

LEARN MORE

Glory, Passion, and Principle by Melissa Lukeman Bohrer (Atria, 2003)
Contains a chapter on Lydia Darragh

"Lydia Barrington Darragh (1728–1789)"
National Women's History Museum
www.nwhm.org/education-resources/biography/biographies/
lydia-barrington-darragh

**Publications [or Publication] of the City History
of Philadelphia** (Published by the City History Society, 1917)
Available on Google Books
Contains a chapter on Lydia Darragh by Henry Darrach

Women and the American Revolution by Mollie Somerville
(National Society, Daughters of the American Revolution, 1974)
Contains a chapter on Lydia Darragh

Women of the American Revolution (Vol. I) by Elizabeth F. Ellet,
contains a chapter on Lydia Darragh (spelled Darrah).
http://archive.org or Google Books

Anna Smith Strong

◆◆◆

PETTICOATS AND HANDKERCHIEFS

Anna Smith Strong could see the waters of Little Bay and Setauket Harbor off New York's Long Island Sound as she hung laundry on her clothesline during the years of the Revolution. She was a 39-year-old woman living with her six children in a small cottage on a family farm in Setauket, a 9.3-square-mile town of farms on the north coast of the Sound. Why would anyone suspect she was aiding a spy ring?

British officers occupied the main house of Anna's farm, confining her family to the cottage. Anna's husband was Setauket's honorable Judge Selah Strong III, a patriot. In 1778 he was accused by the British of resistance to their authority, and he was imprisoned in New York City. Anna's family, like many families in Setauket and other towns, were split in their loyalties. Yet it was through her Tory relatives that Anna was able to arrange her husband's release from imprisonment. By May 1780 he was back in Setauket with the family.

The Strongs, their neighbors, and everyone living on Long Island were surrounded by British soldiers who occupied Long

Selah and Anna Strong's homestead in Setauket, New York, one of the
links in the chain of activity of the Culper Spy Ring.
New-York *magazine, October 1792*

Island after they defeated the Americans in the Battle of Long
Island at the end of August 1776. They stayed until the end of the
Revolution in 1783—seven long years.

While Selah was imprisoned and even after he was released,
Anna tried to carry on her normal activities in Setauket while
British soldiers came and went on horseback, set up camps,
took over homes, or relegated residents like the Strongs to only
certain rooms in their own houses, or demanded residents provide them with food or feed for their horses. They even used
Setauket's Presbyterian Church as a barn and its tombstones in
the church's cemetery as barricades.

Yet within this restrictive environment, Anna is believed to
have been part of the Culper Spy Ring, an espionage operation
instigated by commander in chief George Washington in 1778.
The Culper Spy Ring functioned during a crucial period in the
American Revolution when the British controlled New York
and aimed to divide the colonies by cutting off the northern

ones from the southern ones. To plan his strategy, Washington needed information about British plans, troops, supplies, and more. Setauket was almost 60 miles from New York City, where the British command was headquartered, but Washington called on Major Benjamin Tallmadge to set it up, so the ring was centered in Setauket where the major had grown up. There he could recruit operatives he could trust: his childhood friends. Several of them joined him in the operation and used code names, letters written in invisible ink, and other tricks to pass on clandestine information. One member of the ring would pick up most information then pass it to another, who passed it to another, and finally the intelligence was delivered to George Washington. Anna is said to have been the link between two of the operatives.

In setting up the ring, Tallmadge chose the code name John Bolton for himself and the code number 721 and recruited Abraham Woodhull, a Setauket farmer who was given the code name Samuel Culper Sr. and the code number 722. Woodhull in turn recruited Robert Townsend, who lived in New York City. His code name was Samuel Culper Jr. and his code number was 723. Woodhull also recruited Austin Roe, a Setauket tavern owner. His code number was 724. Another operative was given code number 355, about whom Woodhull had written, "[I] think by the assistance of a 355 of my acquaintance, shall be able to outwit them all." According to Alexander Rose in his 2006 book, *Washington's Spies*, "This mysterious '355'—decoded as 'lady' in the [Culper] Dictionary is mentioned just once in the Culper correspondence. She was Anna Strong." Not everyone agrees. According to Brian Kilmeade and Don Yaeger in their 2013 book, *George Washington's Secret Six*, "In the case of 355 (the "lady" of the Culpers' acquaintance), her code indicates that she was of some degree of social prominence. Was she Anna Smith

Strong . . . [?] A much more likely contender would be a young woman living a fashionable life in New York." A young woman who could have gathered secrets from British officers.

Anna also had contact with many British soldiers. Perhaps she was Agent 355. Perhaps not. Every one of the operatives in the Culper Ring had jobs or responsibilities that made their actions seem logical. In New York City, where most information was gathered, Robert Townsend was a society reporter, which explained why he was out and about gathering information at taverns, coffeehouses, and other spots about goings-on in New York. He also ran a store. Austin Roe quite understandably visited Townsend's store as a customer buying supplies for his tavern. Yet when Townsend packaged the purchased goods, he also included messages written in code and invisible ink. Roe then carried the coded information with him as he rode his horse past the many British soldiers occupying the area, risking discovery on the roads of Long Island.

When he got back to Setauket, Roe stopped by a field on Abraham Woodhull's farm to both tend to his own cows that grazed there and to leave the gathered information in a box on the farm. His actions must have seemed ordinary as well.

Woodhull could likely pick up the information without arousing suspicion, since he was on his own land, and then review it. The next handoff of information, however, was trickier. Woodhull needed to pass it to whaleboat captain Caleb Brewster, code number 725, the next link in the information chain. But Brewster, who was in the Continental Army and commissioned to raid British ships traveling in the waters of Long Island Sound, could be a hard man to find. That's where Anna Smith Strong came in.

Anna was Abraham Woodhull's neighbor and had known him since they were children. He could see her home from his. According to Long Island local historian Beverly C. Tyler, "Since Anna and Selah were close friends with Caleb Brewster, and Brewster didn't want to make direct and frequent contact with Woodhull that might arouse suspicion, letting Anna know where he was hiding his whaleboat was a natural way to operate." Captain Brewster would signal her when he unpredictably arrived at shore and docked in one of the coves.

How did Anna signal Woodhull? According to local lore first detailed by Morton Pennypacker in his book *George Washington's Spies*, with other details added by Kate Strong, the Strong family historian, Anna used her clothesline as a means of communication. When Anna learned of Brewster's arrival, she would hang a black petticoat on her clothesline as a signal to Abraham. To communicate which of the six coves on the shore housed Brewster, Anna hung a number of handkerchiefs: two handkerchiefs meant second cove, and so on. Abraham Woodhull was then able to connect with Captain Brewster to pass on the information. Brewster could then cross the Sound and deliver the information to dragoons (horse-mounted troops) assigned to Major Tallmadge, who was camped with Continental Army troops in various locations. Then a series of dragoons delivered the message to General Washington wherever he was then camped.

According to Beverly C. Tyler, "Folklore is an important ingredient in local history . . . [and] almost always has some basis in fact. The story of Anna and the clothesline . . . can be considered an example of folklore."

As simple and innocent as Anna's clothesline signal method may have seemed to anyone who was watching, she was apparently at risk. A letter from British spy William Heron dated February 4, 1781, indicated that suspicion was increasing. He wrote: "Private dispatches are frequently sent from New York to the Chieftain [General Washington] here by some traitors. They come by way of Setalket [sic], where a certain Brewster receives them at, or near, a certain woman's."

Again, according to Alexander Rose, "the problem [for the British] was that [Captain] Brewster remained at large, and the 'certain woman'—Anna Strong—was untraceable without him."

On one occasion, Brewster, while waiting for Abraham Woodhull, was hiding in Anna Strong's garden when a British lieutenant approached. While Brewster at first thought of roughing him up, he decided against it and let him go. His caution may have saved Anna Strong's life since, Rose observes, Brewster "correctly perceived that if the lieutenant were kidnapped, the British would strengthen their guard in the area, not only casting suspicion on Mrs. Strong . . . but making it still more difficult to pick up Culper letters."

Anna and the Setauket ring escaped that close call, but suspicion was increasing. The Culper Spy Ring began to pull back, but not before providing General Washington with news of a British plan to attack the French fleet, then an ally of the patriot forces.

After the war, when George Washington visited Setauket in April 1790, Selah led his carriage to the party held at Austin Roe's tavern. Anna and Selah lived the rest of their lives in Setauket. Anna died in 1812 and Selah in 1815.

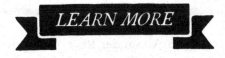

LEARN MORE

"The Culper Spy Ring"
SpyMuseum.com
http://spymuseum.com/dt_portfolio/the-culper-spy-ring

George Washington's Secret Six: The Spy Ring That Saved the American Revolution by Brian Kilmeade and Don Yaeger (Sentinel HC, 2013)

Turn
AMC
www.amctv.com/shows/turn
An AMC series based on the Culper Spy Ring

Washington's Spies: The Story of America's First Spy Ring by Alexander Rose (Bantam Books, 2006)

Dicey Langston

◆◆◆

A WHIG IN A LAND OF TORIES

Sixteen-year-old Dicey Langston was cheeky. Or was she foolish? She was brave. Or was she just rebellious?

Laodicea "Dicey" Langston lived in the Laurens District of South Carolina, an area where most people were Tories or loyalists, those loyal to the British. Dicey was a Whig, a supporter of the Revolution, along with her father, Solomon Langston Sr., who would have been fighting with the militia except for his ill health. Her brother, James, also a Whig, was fighting with the local patriot militia.

But Dicey wanted to work for the Whig cause in her own way. Always alert, she listened to her loyalist neighbors and relatives as she went about her daily activities and was able to learn quite a bit about the goings-on of the British troops. She then communicated this information to her fellow Patriots.

Dicey thought she could get away with her spying, but gradually the loyalists in her community began to suspect her of passing on information. They confronted her father and told him that he would suffer the consequences if she continued and that

81

his property would be in jeopardy. That led to a serious father-daughter talk. The message from Solomon to Dicey: stop!

Dicey did stop her activities until one day she overheard a conversation of a group of Tories who were known for their cruel actions. They were planning to harass her brother, James, and his fellow militiamen, news that prompted Dicey to break her promise to her father and, without telling anyone, sneak out of her house in the dead of night.

Dicey made her way through the wooded area between her home and her brother's camp, trudging through marshes and wading across streams that lacked bridges until she reached the banks of the Tyger River. As she ventured across, the flowing water—up to her waist—swept her along. Unable to see in the darkness, she lost her orientation and floated this way and that, surely fearful of not finding her way or of being harmed by sticks or rocks in the stream. Finally, she made it to the other side, wet and cold.

When Dicey arrived at James's camp, she warned him and his fellow patriot militia soldiers that the Tories planned to attack and urged them to flee and to warn those in the neighborhood.

They didn't respond as she had hoped. James and the others, just back from a maneuver, were tired and hungry and wanted to eat and rest. She urged them to act and perhaps thought of the risks she'd taken to get to their camp. Minutes later though she was cooking pan-fried cornmeal cakes over an open fire in their camp. They shared some, stuck others in their pockets, and only then acted on her alert.

The next day, when the loyalist group arrived at the camp, they found it deserted. By then, Dicey was back at home, above suspicion.

On another occasion, Tories arrived at the Langston home, again with the intention of putting pressure on Dicey's father.

The Tories didn't like the fact that Solomon's sons were militia-men fighting for the Revolution. When one of the men pushed Mr. Langston and pointed a gun at his chest, Dicey shrieked. When the Tory cocked the gun, she leaped forward and stood in front of her father. The gunman screamed at her to move, but she refused. According to one account, "She declared that her own body should receive the ball aimed at his heart!" Then the Tory lowered his gun, put it away, and departed.

In another incident, the tables were turned when Dicey, a Whig, acted to help a Tory. One day when some local Whigs stopped by the Langston family house to rest and feed their horses, she overhead them talking with her father about their plan to visit one of their Tory neighbors with the intention of stealing his horses.

Taking away a man's horse at that time was like taking away his lifeline. Men worked on their horses, fought on their horses,

Dicey Langston protects her father.
Pioneer Mothers of America, *1912*

traveled from one town to another—across long distances, through wooded and swampy areas—on their horses. To steal a man's horses was a great offense.

Both Dicey and her father knew the importance of their neighbor's horses to him. He had never caused the Langstons any trouble despite their being Whigs, and Solomon and Dicey decided to act. Rather than directing Dicey to stop her activities as before, her father urged her to let the neighbor know of the would-be thieves' plan.

While she was at the neighbor's home, though, and after telling him what she had learned, she heard him make plans to call on a group of Tories to capture the Whigs in question. She mounted her horse and then sped back to her home to warn the Whigs of the trap being set for *them*. It was a strange twist: Dicey warned both Whigs and Tories in one day.

On another day, as Dicey was returning from a Whig neighborhood, a group of Tories stopped by her house and wanted her to reveal the information she had picked up on her visit. She wouldn't tell them. When one of the group threatened her with a pistol and warned her that if she didn't cooperate she could be killed, Dicey defiantly took off the scarf that covered her neck, bared part of her bosom as if to point out where he could aim, and said, "Shoot me if you dare. I will not tell you."

As he was about to take her up on her dare, another of the loyalists "threw up his hand, and saved the courageous girl's life."

As the war continued, Dicey was involved in an incident that affected the rest of her life. Some men arrived at her house, introduced themselves as friends of her brother, James, and asked for a rifle he had left with her for safekeeping. As she went to fetch it, she remembered that she had forgotten to ask them for the sign James had given her. By the sign, she would know the request had come from him.

When she returned, she demanded to know the sign. One of the men told her she was too late. With the rifle still in her hand, Dicey pointed it at him and cried, "Do you think so?"

He quickly gave her the sign, laughed, and—acknowledging her strength and spirit—"pronounced her worthy of being the sister of James Langston." Did he linger as he left, and smile? Perhaps. His name was Thomas Springfield, and on January 9, 1783, he married Dicey. The couple lived in Greenville, South Carolina, where he was from, a rural area of forests and rolling hills, and they had 22 children together.

Dicey's obituary appeared in the Greenville, South Carolina, *Mountaineer* on June 10, 1837. It read:

Mrs. Laodicea Springfield, aged 71 years, wife of Thomas Springfield, died on Tuesday, May 23rd. The deceased was the daughter of Solomon Langston of Revolutionary memory, whose family perhaps suffered more from the ruthless ravages of the Tories and Indians than almost any other, and the subject of this remark took an active part in the struggle and performed many daring deeds on behalf of her suffering country and friends. She was the mother of 22 children and has left about 140 grand and great grand children. She was a kind and affectionate wife, mother, and neighbor, and has left a large circle of acquaintances to deplore her loss.

LEARN MORE

Laodicea "Daring Dicey" Langston
www.diceylangston.com

Laodicea Langston—"Daring Dicey"
www.langstonancestry.com/dicey.html

Patriots in Petticoats: Heroines of the American Revolution by
Shirley Raye Redmond (Random House, 2004)

Women of the American Revolution, Vol. I, by Elizabeth F. Ellet,
contains a chapter on Dicey Langston.
http://archive.org or Google Books

Part Three

SABOTEURS

Prudence Wright

◆◆◆

LEADER OF THE PITCHFORK BRIGADE

Prudence and David Wright named their baby, who was born on July 19, 1774, Liberty, a name proclaiming the couple's support for the ideas of the Revolution.

In the months prior to the outbreak of the Revolutionary War at Lexington and Concord, Prudence Wright, like the other women in the small town of Pepperell, Massachusetts—a woodsy town edged by the Nashua River—helped prepare for possible hostilities between pro-Revolutionary families like hers and British soldiers trying to stifle armed conflicts that could lead to war. The women made bullets that soldiers could use in their muskets by melting lead or pewter until it was liquid, then pouring it into molds that formed round balls or bullets. They also poured gunpowder into powder horns that could be easily carried by their soldier husbands.

Prudence's husband, David Wright, was one of Pepperell's minutemen, one of many men in town ready at a minute's notice to respond in case of war. He and the others met often to practice mobilizing and to hone their shooting skills.

Minutemen saying good-bye to their wives as they depart for Lexington.
Dover Publications

On the evening of April 18, 1775, Paul Revere—a Boston silversmith and ardent supporter of the rights of the colonists—rode a horse across the countryside to Lexington, warning residents along his path and to alert fellow revolutionaries John Hancock and Sam Adams that British soldiers were on the way to Lexington and intended to travel to Concord to destroy war supplies and weapons the colonists had hidden there in barns, trees, and other spaces.

Other alarm riders traveled across the countryside throughout the night to spread the news to minutemen and still others and arrived in Pepperell just after sunrise on April 19, 1775. Farmer Abel Parker, who was busy plowing his field, was alerted and "without stopping to unyoke his oxen, ran to the house, and seizing his coat in one hand and his gun in the other, started on a run and did not stop" until he caught up with his fellow minutemen.

The scene was likely the same at the Wright property. Prudence and the children surely watched as David grabbed his gun and ran off as well. As word spread, more and more fathers and sons, muskets in hand, on their own and in companies, crowded the country roads leading to Lexington and Concord.

What would happen next? That was on the minds of everyone in Pepperell, including Prudence and her children. Couriers alerted them of unfolding events. Prudence and others heard that shots had been fired by both sides on Lexington Green, a grassy area in Lexington that was used as a training area for the militia. They heard that the British had marched through Concord on their retreat to Boston and that many people had been killed. It was a scary time.

Rumors were flying in Pepperell and surrounding towns about possible threats. What were the British plans? Did the British have spies in and around town listening for information they could provide to the British command? No one knew for sure. Prudence didn't know either.

The Battle of Lexington.
Dover Publications

Prudence Cummings was born on November 26, 1740, in Hollis, Massachusetts, about eight miles from Pepperell. She was the daughter of Samuel Cummings, the first town clerk of Hollis, and his wife, Prudence Lawrence. Her older sisters, Mary and Sibbell, were born six and four years before her. Prudence was two when her brother Samuel was born, and she was five when Thomas was born. The day after her 17th birthday, she welcomed her youngest brother, Benjamin, into the family.

A few days after Christmas, on December 28, 1761, when she was 21, she married David Wright of Pepperell. Two years later, their first child, David, was born on March 28, 1763, followed within nine years by five more children.

Prudence made a home for all of them and went about the ordinary tasks of colonial-era life—knitting socks, preserving meat, dipping and molding candles, and boiling sap to make sugary sweets. She excelled in the art of sand scouring, a way of cleaning her wooden floor in the time before floors were sealed with paint. Once the floor was clean and washed and while it was still damp, Prudence would scour it with sand to make it smooth, as did other women. Yet she was known for her ability to also use the sand to create lovely patterns on the living room floor.

In the wake of the attack on Lexington and Concord, though, Prudence had other concerns. There was a war of sorts going on in her birth family. Two of her brothers, Samuel and Thomas, along with their friend Leonard Whiting, were suspected of being Tories—supporters of the British who opposed independence for the colonies.

When Prudence went to her family home in Hollis to visit her widowed mother, her brothers were there when she arrived, speaking with their friend Leonard. As Prudence chatted with her mother, she overheard bits of the men's conversation, including talk of spies who would be passing from Canada down to Boston and delivering useful information to the British troops. Then she overheard Leonard talk of making plans to "meet a force of English and lead them to Groton," a town a few miles south.

Alarmed by his comment, and aware that Groton was nearby and that the road leading from Canada to Boston ran through Pepperell, Prudence returned to Pepperell and shared her information with her friends, women who, like her, supported the boycott of British goods, spun their own yarn, wove their own cloth, and drank tea made of basil leaves and other herbs instead of tea imported from England.

As far as the women were concerned, if they could help it, no one was going to go through Pepperell carrying messages to the British. They decided to gather and spread the word from house to house throughout Pepperell and nearby towns.

Thirty to forty women met and chose Prudence as their commander. Prudence, in turn, chose Mrs. Job Shattuck as her lieutenant—the use of military titles was an indication of how seriously they took their concerns. History has preserved the names of only a few of the others. The group came to be known as Mrs. David Wright's Guard.

After hatching a plan, the women went to their homes and exchanged their clothes for those of their husbands, fathers, or brothers. They wanted to appear as if they were men. They armed themselves with muskets, pitchforks, and such other weapons as they could find and set off for what was called Jewett's Bridge over the Nashua River in Pepperell.

It was dark when they reached the bridge. As they waited, holding their muskets and pitchforks, hidden by the surrounding high land and the curve of the road ahead from anyone who

Bridge over the Nashua River in Pepperell.
Courtesy of the Pepperell Historical Commission

approached, Prudence and the other women must have wondered who they would encounter but probably expected to meet
a force of soldiers as big as their group.

What happened next? It depends on which story you read.
In one version that appeared in the 1848 book *The History of the
Town of Groton* by Caleb Butler, "Soon there appeared one on
horseback, one supposed to be treasonably engaged in convey-
ing intelligence to the enemy." He was "immediately arrested,
unhorsed, searched, and the treasonable correspondence found
concealed in his boots."

Butler also stated that the women were "resolutely determined, that no foe to freedom, foreign or domestic, should pass
that bridge." Who was the spy? Not a stranger. He was Leonard
Whiting, the friend of Prudence's brothers, the very one who

had been talking to her brothers at the Cummings family home about meeting "a force of English."

In 1899 Mary L. P. Shattuck presented two other versions of the story in a speech and later in a publication titled *Prudence Wright and the Women Who Guarded the Bridge: The Story of Jewett's Bridge, Pepperell, Massachusetts, 1775*. In Shattuck's first version, which she attributed to a descendant of Prudence and David Wright, as the women waited by the bridge, two horsemen appeared. Prudence ordered them to halt. When they tried to get away, the women "seized the reins of their horses."

Again, one of the riders was Captain Leonard Whiting, Prudence's brother's friend. He pulled out his gun and was set to use it when the other rider said, "I recognize Prude's voice and she would wade through blood for the rebel cause." It was Prudence's brother Samuel. Whiting put away his gun. "The men were dismounted and searched, and despatches from the British forces to the British general in Boston were found upon them." The women surrounded them and walked with the two men the six miles "to Groton to the Committee of Safety, and the next day [the men] were given their liberty on condition that they would leave the colony. They departed in the direction of New York. Samuel Cummings never returned. Samuel was the favorite brother of Prudence, and his loss was a life-long grief to her."

A descendant of Leonard Whiting told a different story in the second version related by Shattuck. In it, as the women waited and talked, the two men approaching the bridge heard the women before they saw them. One of them recognized his sister's voice. His thoughts and feelings were related in an 1898 poem by Annie V. Cuthbertson:

> *Not one further step I ride!*
> *One who rode with Whiting cried*

'Tis my sister Prue! Alas,
She would never let me pass
Save when her dead body fell!
I turn back from Pepperell

Yet, it wasn't Samuel. It was "her brother Thomas [who] was never seen again by his family or townsmen, so this tradition runs."

Whiting, however, not so easily scared off, rode into the throng of women, or so this version of the story goes. According to Shattuck, "The women surrounded him, seized his horse, and at the command of 'Capt. Wright,' compelled him to dismount and submit to search. In his boots were found treasonable papers."

Then the women "marched their prisoner to the middle of the town, probably up Main Street to the tavern kept by one Solomon Rogers. They were entertained—a substantial supper no doubt—and guarded their prisoner until morning, when they marched him to Groton and delivered him into custody. The papers were sent to the Committee of Safety at Charlestown."

While the two versions related by Shattuck differ as to which of Prudence's brothers accompanied Whiting that night, *History of the Town of Hollis, N.H.* by Samuel T. Worcester in 1879 notes that almost a year after the events at the bridge, both Samuel and Thomas Cummings were brought to trial in Hollis, suspected by their "fellow townsmen to be loyalists or Tories as opposed to the independence of the colonies." That contradicts both of the versions related by Mary Shattuck, which state that one brother or the other departed immediately after the bridge incident and wasn't seen again. That being said, after the trial, which didn't favor either brother, both Samuel and Thomas Cummings did leave Hollis, deserting their families, and neither ever returned.

Some time later, Prudence's other brother, 17-year-old Benjamin, who was pro-Revolution, fought at the Battle of Bunker Hill.

In the years during the war and after, Prudence and David had four more children—11 in all. Their oldest son, David, fought in the last years of the Revolution. Prudence died in Pepperell in 1823 at the age of 83.

Marker for Mrs. David Wright's Guard.
Courtesy of the Pepperell Historical Commission

A poem about the women, written by Susan H. Wixon of Fall River, appeared in the November 1899 issue of *American Monthly* magazine, 124 years after the events at Jewett's Bridge.

———————•———————

The women over field and farm
Kept faithful watch and ward;
Shielded the town from ev'ry harm,
Nor thought their duty hard.
They guarded bridge and forest wood—
These women fair and slight;
And for the right they ever stood,
At morning, noon and night.
The story of their gallant feat
Flew swift o'er hill and dell;
And "Reg'lars" then, cared not to meet
Prudence of Pepperell.
Their country's honor, in an hour
Most serious and grave,
Was thus upheld with grace and power,
By women true and brave.
And on the scroll where heroes' names
Appear in shining light;
With names our country proudly claims,
Gleams that of Prudence Wright.

LEARN MORE

History of the Town of Groton, Including Pepperell and Shirley by
Caleb Butler (Press of T. R. Marvin, 1848)
https://archive.org/details/historyoftownofg00butl

"Town Meeting dated: March 19, 1777"
Pepperell Historical Commission
www.pepperell-mass.com/150/Revolutionary-War---5

Prudence Wright and the Women Who Guarded the Bridge:
The Story of Jewett's Bridge, Pepperell, Massachusetts, 1775 by
Mary L. P. Shattuck, 1912
www.pepperellhistory.org or www.pepperellcoveredbridge
.org/wp-content/uploads/2010/06/The_Women_who
_Guarded_the_Bridge.pdf

Sybil Ludington

❖❖❖

ON STAR UNDER THE STARS

The British were coming! But 16-year-old Sybil Ludington couldn't have known it was happening. It was 4:00 in the afternoon of April 25, 1777. Sybil might have been helping her mother prepare supper, feeding her horse, Star, or interacting with her seven younger brothers and sisters—Rebecca, 14, Mary, 12, Archie, 9, Henry, 8, Derick, 6, Tertulus, 4, and Abigail, 1.

Sybil, born April 5, 1761, couldn't have known that 20 transports and six war vessels carrying 2,000 British troops had sailed into Long Island Sound and dropped anchor in the mouth of the Saugatuck River in Compo, just 30 miles from the home where she lived with her family in Fredericksburg, New York.

Colonel Henry Ludington, Sybil's father, couldn't have known it was happening either. Or that General William Tryon was leading the troops. Colonel Ludington had served under him during the French and Indian Wars when he was fighting for the British. Now Henry Ludington was on the other side, one of those fighting for independence from the rule of England's King George III.

Sybil Ludington Monument (**Carmel, NY**). *Photo by Susan Casey*

At the start of the Revolution, Ludington was aide-de-camp to General George Washington. Later he became commander of a militia of 400 men in western New York, where he lived. He didn't know he'd be called on to lead his men to fight against the arriving troops. Neither did Sybil.

As a commander, Colonel Ludington was important to the Revolution. The British offered a reward for his capture, dead or alive. Many Tories wanted to collect the reward, so the colonel and the entire family, living on a farm in the countryside, had to be on guard. Sybil (whose name is sometimes spelled Sebal or Sibbell), the oldest of his eight (at the time of the ride and 12 in all) children, was often his sentinel.

One night when Sybil and her younger sister Rebecca were standing watch, guns in hand, they discovered that a group of

Tories had surrounded the house. Fearful but quick-thinking, Sybil and Rebecca quickly roused their four brothers and two other sisters, gave them candles, and told them to walk back and forth in front of the windows in every room in the house. The moving silhouettes created by the candlelight gave the Tories the impression that the house was heavily guarded, so they didn't dare attack. Sybil and her sister had outwitted them.

While Sybil couldn't have known about the present danger only miles from her home, locals near the shore, hidden behind trees and rocks, watched the British soldiers—some in red coats with epaulettes, some in bright yellow breeches and black boots—exit the ships, get into formation, and march north led by General Tryon, formerly the royal governor of New York, and his assistants, Generals James Tanner Agnew and William Erskine.

The locals might not have known where the troops were headed or what they planned to do but they surely understood that something was bound to happen. A messenger hurried to alert General Gold Selleck Silliman, who lived in Fairfield and was in command of the militia in that part of Connecticut. Silliman sent news to General David Wooster and General Benedict Arnold, both in New Haven, to bring their troops to meet him. Couriers were sent to nearby towns to alert them, and a messenger on horseback trod through heavily wooded terrain to tell Colonel Ludington to gather his militia to join the defense.

Silliman at first guessed that the troops planned to attack Redding, Connecticut, 13 miles north. He gathered his men and headed in that direction. That guess turned out to be wrong. The British continued marching north and camped for the night in Weston, about eight miles north. Any local who guessed that their true destination was Danbury, Connecticut, a town of about 400 homes roughly 20 miles north of the shore, would have been right.

In the morning the British continued on with no resistance, intent on arriving in Danbury to destroy the supplies the Revolutionary Army stored there, including 5,000 pairs of shoes and stockings, a printing press, hospital bedding, thousands of bushels of grain, hundreds of barrels of beef and pork, and more than 1,000 tents. Loss of the supplies would be disastrous to the Revolutionary forces. Without them, how could they wage war against the British? That's why Tryon wanted to destroy them.

The next day—Saturday, April 26—the British troops made their way closer to Danbury where men, women, and children were fleeing town, fearful of what the approaching troops might do to those loyal to the Revolution. Some pulled oxcarts and wagons filled with their possessions along rutted roads out of town. Some hid in the woods or in barns. Others secreted horses and cattle in the nearby forests. Some hid their young sons because of rumors that the troops had plans to kill young boys before they could grow up to be soldiers. Some stayed in town to guard their homes.

Danbury needed a defense. Only 50 Continental Army soldiers usually guarded the town, but they were away. A militia of only 100 men was no match for the thousands of troops marching toward them. While every family had a musket, many were torn between defending their families or the town. Those loyal to the king, the Tories, stayed put.

The sun was shining as the British troops reached Danbury between 2:00 and 3:00 on that Saturday afternoon. General Tryon wasn't hesitant about settling in. Since he planned to stay the night, he first took over a house, that of Nehemiah Dibble, as his headquarters.

Generals Erskine and Agnew, riding their horses on Main Street, flanked by many other mounted soldiers, were looking for quarters for themselves when, according to *History of Danbury, Connecticut, 1684–1896* by James Montgomery Bailey, an older man named Silas Hamilton, worried about the fate of a bolt of cloth he'd left at a town shop, raced on his horse to the shop in hopes of retrieving it. Perhaps he was fearful that the shop would be burned by the British troops. He dismounted, ran into the store, and then ran quickly out, cloth in hand. Silas mounted his horse and held the reins with one hand and the bolt of cloth with the other as he was quickly pursued by a half-dozen troopers. One of the troopers shouted and swung a sword at him. Silas, surely terrified, lost his hold on the cloth and it unraveled, flying out behind him, scaring the pursuing horses and allowing him to safely ride away.

Others in Danbury were not so lucky. When four young men hiding in a house fired on the troops, the building was torched and the men inside died. As other British troops reached the courthouse, they discharged their artillery, sending heavy cannon balls flying up the street, terrifying families hiding in their homes.

The British had made their point. When troops found supplies in several buildings, locals didn't try to stop them. One building full of stored grain was burned to the ground. Another that contained barrels of meat was set on fire and "fat from the burning meat ran ankle-deep in the street."

In late afternoon, storm clouds filled the sky and it began to rain, a condition that surely complicated the journey of troops led by Generals Silliman, Wooster, and Arnold and muddied the roads traveled by the messenger on his way to the Ludington farm.

At around 9:00 PM the messenger finally arrived at the Ludington farm and greeted Colonel Ludington with the news that the British were burning Danbury. The messenger told him to muster his militia, a task that Ludington knew would take hours. The 400 men in his militia regiment had earlier returned home to plant their spring crops. Their farms were widely scattered across miles and miles of the countryside. It would take hours to rouse them. How could Colonel Ludington do it himself and be at his home to organize the men when they arrived? He turned to the exhausted messenger for help, but the messenger told him he was too tired to go. According to Willis Fletcher Johnson in his 1907 book, *Colonel Henry Ludington: A Memoir,*

> In this emergency, he turned to his daughter Sybil, who, a few days before, had passed her 16th birthday, and bade her to take a horse, ride for the men, and tell them to be at his house by daybreak. One who even rides now from Carmel to Cold Spring will find rugged and dangerous roads with lonely stretches. Imagination only can picture what it was like a century and a quarter ago, on a dark night.

Sybil mounted her horse, Star, surely watched by Colonel Ludington and the messenger as she departed. Though it was raining, her way was lit when the moon shone through the storm clouds.

It was a dangerous mission, an almost 40-mile ride. Thieves and ruffians were known to be in the forests, waiting to steal from or attack those who passed. As the rain beat down, Sybil must have feared for her safety as she steered Star alongside the middle branch of the Croton River on the way to the town of Carmel. When she arrived she gave the warning: "The British are burning Danbury!" The village bell began ringing to alert the town militia to muster. "Tell them to join my father at Ludington's Mill," she said, and off she went along the paths edging Lake Carmel, then along the shore of Lake Gleneida. She banged on the doors of the scattered farmhouses with a stick, telling each person who answered the same message: "The British are burning Danbury. Join my father at Ludington's Mill. Tell your neighbors."

As Sybil rode on, the British troops continued their assault on the supplies stowed in Danbury. In one building they found bottles of wine and rum. Before torching the building, they began drinking the spirits. Not long after:

> the greater part of the force were in a riotous state of drunkenness . . . the drunken men went up and down the Main Street in squads, singing army songs, shouting coarse speeches, hugging each other, swearing, yelling, and otherwise conducting themselves as becomes an invader when he is very, very drunk. . . . The carousers tumbled down here and there as they advanced in the stages of drunkenness.

Fearful townspeople peered out their windows at the chaos. Meanwhile, Sybil, still traveling on the narrow paths through the forests and past the dark farm fields, was most likely having a harder time of it. Most people had extinguished the lights in their homes. She would have had to be cautious in steering Star and on guard against cowboys and skinners who were known to hide in the woods to rob or even kill those who passed.

Meanwhile, in Danbury, General Tryon, who had planned to stay the night and "spend the Sabbath leisurely in Danbury," was at his quarters when he got news around 1:00 in the morning on April 27 "that the rebels under Wooster and Arnold had reached Bethel," which was only three or more miles away. He ordered that the drunken and sleeping men be roused.

Yet he didn't order his troops to leave town. Instead he ordered them to go about destroying their foe. Houses marked with a cross, the indication that the occupants were Tories— supporters of the British—were passed by and others randomly burned. "Flames seemed to burst out simultaneously in all directions. . . . An old lady afterward said that if she had not been so frightened, she could have put out the newly kindled fire with a pail of water."

As 19 homes as well as some stores and shops burned, the sky turned orange. Could Sybil see the flames lighting up the sky as she raced through the countryside, continuing on to Kent Fields and then to Redding Corners, enduring the rain, the darkness, the fear of attack, and her own fatigue? By then, militiamen she had summoned had begun arriving at Ludington's Mill.

Signs mark the route taken by Sybil Ludington.
Photo by Susan Casey

ACCOLADES FOR SYBIL LUDINGTON

———————•———————

In 1935 the New York State Education Department placed a series of roadside signs that mark the route Sybil Ludington took when she helped muster her father's militia.

In 1961 sculptor Anna Hyatt Huntington created a statue of Sybil, depicting the ardent, active young woman on horseback, intent on her task. The original full-size statue is in Carmel, a town along her route, and a smaller replica stands in Danbury. Another smaller original of the statue is on display in the Daughters of the American Revolution Museum in Washington, DC.

For the celebration of the bicentennial of the United States, Sybil Ludington was depicted on a postage stamp issued by the US Postal Service in 1975 as one of the Contributors to the Cause stamps in the United States Bicentennial Series. It was an apt description. Sybil willingly and bravely did contribute to the cause.

General Tryon, leaving Danbury aflame, then began leading the retreat of his troops toward their ships. Suspecting correctly that the American troops would be positioned along the route he had taken to get to Danbury, Tryon, with the aid of local Tories, took an alternate route. Locals tried to impede his progress by destroying a bridge, and through other acts.

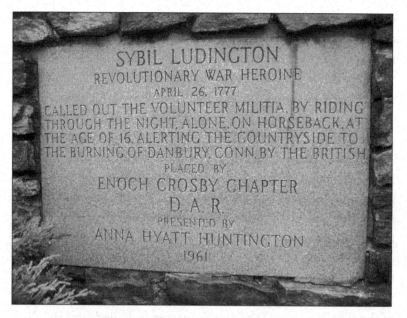

Gravestone of Sybil Ludington.
Photo by Val Riordan

The American generals split their forces, with Wooster sending Arnold and Silliman to Ridgefield while he headed north of that town and encountered Tryon and his troops while they were eating breakfast. The Battle of Ridgefield ensued. In the fighting, General Wooster was hit in the back by a musket ball and died. While the troops of Generals Silliman and Arnold, along with those of Colonel Ludington, pursued the British as they retreated, locals also pitched in by shooting troops while hiding behind bushes and trees. According to an article that appeared in the *Connecticut Journal*, "The enemy's loss is judged to be more than double our numbers, and about twenty prisoners."

Skirmishes continued until the British were aboard their ships. By then, Sybil was likely asleep in her bed after her long ride the night before. Sybil's contribution was acknowledged in

Colonel Henry Ludington: A Memoir: "There is no extravagance in comparing her ride with that of Paul Revere and its midnight message. Nor was her errand less efficient than his."

After the war, Sybil lived with her parents until, at age 23, she married Edmond Ogden. Their only child, Henry, born in 1786, was only 13 when Edmond died of yellow fever. After his death, Sybil bought and operated a tavern in Catskill, New York, and when she sold it six years later for three times the purchase price, she bought Henry—by then an attorney—and his wife and child a home in Unadilla, New York. She lived there with them for the next 30 years, grandmother to their four sons and two daughters.

But Henry preceded his mother in death, and without means of support, Sybil applied for a government pension. Although Sybil proved beyond a doubt that she was the wife of a veteran of the Revolutionary War, her request was denied, and she died less than six months later. Sybil was buried next to her parents. Her gravestone reads: IN MEMORY OF SIBBELL LUDINGTON, WIFE OF EDMOND OGDEN.

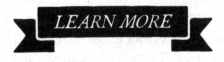

LEARN MORE

Colonel Henry Ludington: A Memoir by Willis Fletcher Johnson (Self-published, printed by his grandchildren Lavinia Elizabeth Ludington and Charles Henry Ludington, 1907)

Glory, Passion, and Principle: The Story of Eight Remarkable Women at the Core of the American Revolution by Melissa Lukeman Bohrer (Simon and Schuster, 2003)
Contains a chapter on Sybil Ludington

"New York Patriot" by V. T. Dacquino
www.archives.nysed.gov/apt/magazine/archivesmag
_spring07.pdf

Sybil Ludington: The Call to Arms by V. T. Dacquino (Purple Mountain Press, 2000)

Mary Lindley Murray

WINE, CAKE, AND A GETAWAY

Could hosting a party help the Revolution? Prevent a battle? If only we could ask Mary.

Mary Lindley Murray and her husband, Robert Murray, were known for their parties. One was, according to an 1894 account, "a grand public breakfast . . . in honor of the Tunisian Ambassador." At the party, "nearly thirty people all decked out in their imposing robes" strolled through the spacious rooms of Mary and Robert's two-story home on a 29-acre estate in New York City. Guests caught glimpses of the ambassador, who wore a turban, sported a long beard, and wore a "silk jacket . . . embroidered in gold." The chronicler described how "mirth and pleasure echoed through the hall."

But on September 15, 1776, Mary hosted a simpler party. Some British generals stopped by for wine and cake.

Mary seems to have had the right personality for a hostess, as described by her son in 1850's *Women of the American Revolution*: "My mother was a woman of amiable disposition, and

Mary Lindley Murray entertaining British soldiers on her porch during the American Revolution.
Library of Congress, LC-USZ62-20969

remarkable for mildness, humanity and liberality of sentiment. She was indeed a faithful and affectionate wife, a tender mother."

The atmosphere on September 15, 1776, though, was hardly conducive to a party of any sort. British and American troops had been fighting for control of New York City for weeks. The British were winning. The Americans were retreating.

Mary was at home, perhaps with her daughters, Susannah and Beulah. Robert was away. The windows of Mary's two-story home overlooked Kips Bay on the East River. The night before, British ships had sailed into the bay. Two of them, the *Phoenix* and the *Roebuck*, sported 44 guns each.

On shore, 500 patriot militiamen waited to defend the area. When the British demonstrated their naval superiority by firing from ships, 15-year-old Continental Army soldier Private Joseph

Plumb Martin was stunned. He later wrote, "all of a sudden there came such a peal of thunder from British Shipping that I thought my head would go with the sound. I made a frog's leap for the ditch and lay as still as I possibly could and began to consider which part of my carcass would go first."

After Joseph and many of his fellow soldiers ran for it, about 4,000 British Army troops under the command of General William Howe landed on the shore. There was havoc. Commander in chief George Washington, already at his camp in Harlem Heights, heard the sounds of the cannons, mounted his horse, and galloped there. He was so upset by the quick retreat of the patriots that "he plunged his horse among them, trying to stop them," but to no avail. Washington soon retreated and returned to his camp. The British had won. The last of the Continental Army troops heading out of the city were led by Major General Israel Putnam.

What did Mary see or hear that morning? What side was she on? Who was she rooting for?

Mary Lindley was born in 1726 and raised in Pennsylvania, the daughter of Thomas Lindley, a blacksmith who had moved from Ireland to Pennsylvania in 1719. Thomas Lindley was a Quaker, a member of a religious group that believed in neutrality in time of war. With other Quakers, he started a company called Durham Furnace, a successful venture that Mary may have visited as a girl and seen its forges and furnaces and its production of iron stoves, tools, and pots.

Mary's father was a man of influence, connected with men of power and sway in Pennsylvania. She witnessed him being appointed justice of the peace in 1738 and receiving an appointment to the Pennsylvania Assembly a year later.

Mary met Robert Murray, one of her family's neighbors. He was an Irish-born merchant who was a descendant of a noble Scottish family. His roots were in England, but he sought his fortune in America and was successful, due in part to connections with influential merchants he met through Mary's father. When he wanted to marry Mary, he abandoned his religion and became a Quaker. The two married in 1744, a year after Mary's father died.

Years before the outbreak of the Revolution, Robert Murray was trading goods in places as far-flung as the West Indies, selling flour and wheat from the Pennsylvania mills. Later, the family moved to New York, where Robert's business also thrived.

Both Robert and Mary were Quakers, understood to be neutral in times of war. Yet when tensions began increasing between the British and the colonists in the early 1770s, they had their leanings. Robert was thought to be a loyalist, sympathetic to the British cause due to his many British business connections. Members of Mary's family served on both sides. While Mary was apparently loyal to her husband, she was also thought to be sympathetic to the struggle for independence.

How did Mary's sympathy with the Whigs—supporters of the Revolution—play a part on that chaotic day of September 15, 1776? Or did it?

As Major General Israel Putnam was leading his 3,500 troops, a third of the Continental Army, out of town, he was cautious. He knew his troops would be no match for the well-trained British Army or their hired mercenary troops (the Hessians from Germany) who were heading into New York City to join the other victorious troops. Putnam didn't want to get cornered by them, trapped on the southern end of Manhattan Island. Only the day before, a British officer had written of one patriot soldier who had encountered a Hessian soldier in New York: "I saw a

Hessian sever a rebel's head from his body and clap it on a pole in the entrenchments."

To avoid meeting the British troops, Putnam led his troops northward along a road that edged the North (Hudson) River to a fork that would connect to another road on which he and his troops could safely march and then rejoin the rest of the Continental Army troops in Harlem Heights.

This turned out to be a bad plan. According to a military journal kept at the time by Dr. James Thacher, a surgeon in the Continental Army, "It so happened that a body of about eight-thousand British and Hessians were at the same moment advancing on the road, which would have brought them in immediate contact with General Putnam, before he could have reached the turn onto the other road."

Enter Mary Lindley Murray. Sir Henry Clinton, the commander of the 8,000 British troops marching to join other British forces, approached Mary's house. It was on a hill, today called Murray Hill, at East 37th Street and Park Avenue in New York City. He saw the "magnificent avenue of elms" that led to Mary and Robert's "spacious, square-built mansion" and stopped.

Israel Putnam.
The Pictorial Field-Book of the Revolution,
by Benson J. Lossing, 1860

So Mary hosted a party. She and two of her daughters, Susannah and Beulah, entertained the officers. Dr.

Thacher's journal continues, "Mrs. Murray treated them with cake and wine, and by means of her refreshments and agreeable conversation, beguiled them to stay a couple of hours."

Meanwhile, Putnam and his troops trudged on, came to a turn in the road, and soon were united with Washington and the rest of the Continental Army.

During the two-hour party, one of the officers, Governor Tryon, clearly aware of Mary's support of the Revolution "[was] joking her about her American friends." Mary, one author noted, "might have turned the laugh on him; for one half hour, it is said, would have enabled the British to secure the road at the turn, and cut off Putnam's retreat."

With a capture of 3,500 Continental Army troops so close at hand, why did Clinton stop? As it turns out, British general William Howe had ordered Clinton to stop in that area until the rest of the British troops arrived later in the day.

Yet the question remains: Did Mary play a part in this? Little evidence exists, but at the time, there was popular conjecture. Five days after Mary's party, on September 20, 1776, Dr. Thacher wrote of the event in his journal:

> Most fortunately, the British generals, seeing no prospect of engaging our troops, halted their own, and repaired to the house of Mr. Robert Murray. . . . Mrs. Murray treated them with cake and wine, and they were induced to tarry two hours or more. By this happy incident, General Putnam, by continuing his march, escaped a reencounter with a greatly superior force, which must have proved fatal to his whole party. One half hour, it is said, would have been sufficient for the enemy to have secured the road at the turn, and entirely cut off General Putnam's retreat. It has since become

almost a common saying among our officers, that Mrs. Murray saved this part of the American army.

Six years later, on Christmas Day, 1782, Mary died. Her husband, Robert, died four years later. Their firstborn child, Lindley Murray, a grammarian and author of 11 textbooks, was the best-selling author in the world in the first half of the 19th century with sales of some 20 million books, the most popular being *English Reader*, a book praised by Abraham Lincoln. Robert and Mary had 12 other children, but only five lived to be adults.

MARY LINDLEY MURRAY ON BROADWAY?

In the 1920s, nearly 150 years after Mrs. Murray entertained British officers at her home, New York had become a sophisticated, hip, lively city of tall buildings, nightclubs, and theaters. Yet Mary Lindley Murray had not been forgotten. A plaque honoring her was nestled in the ivy of a median park where the Murray home once stood, on the corner of East 37th Street and Park Avenue.

One day in the 1920s, songwriters Richard Rodgers, Lorenz Hart, and librettist Herbert Fields, who collaborated on many Broadway musicals, were walking by that corner. The plaque caught their eye. Mary's story gave them an idea for a musical comedy, which evolved into

Dearest Enemy. It opened on Broadway on September 18, 1925, at the Knickerbocker Theatre.

A playwright named Robert E. Sherwood was also inspired by the story and penned *Small War on Murray Hill,* a comedy that opened in 1957 at the Ethel Barrymore Theatre in New York City. In that version of her story Mary not only offered General William Howe

cake and wine, but also, in order to stall him, then prompted him to enjoy a hot bath, a glass of wine, dinner, and a brandy while Putnam and his troops got away.

Surrounded by busy streets and tall buildings, a plaque honoring Mary Lindley Murray reads: IN HONOR OF MARY LINDLEY MURRAY / WIFE OF ROBERT MURRAY / FOR SERVICES RENDERED HER COUNTRY DURING THE AMERICAN REVOLUTION, ENTERTAINING AT HER HOME, ON THIS SITE, GEN. HOWE AND HIS OFFICERS, UNTIL THE AMERICAN TROOPS UNDER GEN. PUTNAM ESCAPED.
Photo by Susan Casey

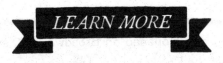

Dearest Enemy, 1925, "Here in My Arms"
www.dailymotion.com/video/
x1hnn7g_dearest-enemy-1925-here-in-my-arms_music

In the Olden Time: A Short History of the Descendants of John Murray the Good by Sarah Murray (Steftner, Lambert & Co., 1894)

A Military Journal During the American Revolutionary War, from 1775 to 1783 by James Thacher, MD (Cotton & Barnard, 1823)
https://archive.org or Google Books

The Murrays of Murray Hill by Charles Monaghan (Urban History, 1998)

Grace and Rachel Martin

◆◆◆

MASQUERADING HOSTESSES

Grace Waring Martin and Rachel Clay Martin were young and fearless. The sisters-in-law were the wives of two sons in the Martin family. While their husbands were away fighting with the militia, Grace and Rachel, too, became involved—not on a battlefield but on a road near the family home.

When she was only 14, Grace Waring married William Martin. Rachel Clay, the first cousin of Henry Clay (a lawyer who represented Kentucky in both the Senate and in the House of Representatives) married William's brother, Barkley Martin. The husbands were two of the eight children of Elizabeth Marshall and Abram Martin. The parents had both grown up in Caroline County and after their marriage settled near the town of Ninety Six in South Carolina, an area on the boundary of the land settled by farmers and the land inhabited by the Cherokee nation. Most of the settlers, like the Martins, were pioneers from other states. It was in Ninety Six that Abram and Elizabeth raised their seven sons and one daughter, Letty.

When the war broke out and the local militia asked for volunteers, Elizabeth said to her sons, "Go boys, fight for your country! Fight till death, if you must, but never let your country be dishonored. Were I a man I would go with you." All seven of her sons joined the fight.

The Martin family home where Grace and Rachel were living with Elizabeth while their husbands were fighting with the militia was located in a dangerous area. A war was being waged between the Whigs and the Tories. Neighbors on either side of the conflict not only disagreed but took action to ruin each other's farms, steal each other's animals, and more. One neighbor even tarred and feathered another because of a disagreement about the war.

With the men away, Grace, Rachel, and Elizabeth, pro-Revolution women, were fearful of attacks by local Tories. Elizabeth Martin had previously been the target of such an attack. Tories had visited her home and slashed open her feather beds, which were a luxury cherished by South Carolina settlers. When her sons came home, bringing with them a wounded Continental Army soldier, Elizabeth asked them to pursue and punish the Tories. The young men departed but left the wounded soldier with Elizabeth. When Tories heard of this and came to take the soldier, Elizabeth successfully hid him from them. And so it continued: Tory versus Whig; Whig versus Tory.

One night, though, it was Whig versus the British. Grace and Rachel Martin heard that a courier carrying papers to be delivered to British officers commanding forces in the area would be traveling on a road through the heavily forested area near their home. The courier's escort would be two British officers.

Could Grace and Rachel prevent delivery of the papers? They decided to try.

Grace and Rachel surely knew that what they were planning was dangerous, but they had something at stake. The plans being carried by the courier might be related to activities in which their husbands were involved. The women knew as well that plans were constantly changing—depending on circumstances, weather, geography, available equipment or ammunition, or news of troop movements or locations. They also knew that messages were often carried by men or women on horseback.

One source, *The Pioneer Mothers of America* by Harry Clinton Green and Mary Wolcott Green, suggests a conversation that might have taken place between the sisters-in-law.

"Grace," said Mrs. Rachel banteringly, "if you were a soldier's wife, I'd dare you to join me in capturing that courier and his papers for General Greene."

"Soldier's wife," said Mrs. Grace scornfully, "I dare do anything you can do."

The plan quickly matured.

Grace and Rachel's plan was to seize the papers and send them to Major Nathanael Greene, commander of the Continental Army in the Southern Campaign.

At Elizabeth's house, Grace and Rachel rifled through clothing left by their husbands and dressed themselves to look like militiamen. "With rifles over their shoulders and pistols in their belts," they exited the house.

It was dark. They quietly made their way to the side of the road they knew the men would travel on. They hid behind bushes and trees that edged the road and waited. For some time it was silent except for the ordinary sounds of the forested land at night.

Meanwhile, at the Martin home, their mother-in-law, Elizabeth, saw the courier and soldiers pass by her house.

Grace and Rachel must soon have heard them as well. According to Elizabeth Ellet, author of *Women of the American Revolution*, who in the early 1800s interviewed ancestors and friends about the women who participated in the Revolution, "As they came close to the spot, the disguised women leaped from their covert in the bushes, presented their pistols at the officers, and demanded the instant surrender of the party and their despatches. The men were completely taken by surprise, and in their alarm at the sudden attack, yielded a prompt submission."

Grace and Rachel Martin intercept courier.
Pioneer Mothers of America, *1912*

Then Grace and Rachel demanded the men accept parole—an agreement by the men not to take up arms against the Americans or encourage others to do so in exchange for their release. The men signed a paper agreeing to the parole, then rode back in the direction they had come.

Grace and Rachel returned home via a shortcut through the woods, then changed from their husbands' clothes into their own. A bit later, when Elizabeth heard a knock at the door, she opened it to see the courier and the two soldiers. Grace and Rachel might have been wondering if the soldiers had discovered that they'd been tricked.

Elizabeth greeted the men and recognized them as those she had seen ride by earlier. She asked, according to Ellet, why they were "returning so soon after they had passed. They replied by showing their paroles, saying they had been taken prisoners by two rebel lads."

The conversation continued as the two young wives asked the men if they were armed and, if so, why they hadn't used their weapons. The officers admitted to having been taken off guard and said that the confrontation had happened so quickly they didn't have time to grab and use their guns.

Yet why had the men stopped? They wanted a place to stay for the night, they said. Satisfied with their explanation, Elizabeth let them in.

Did Grace and Rachel sleep well that night? We'll never know. According to Ellet, the soldiers "departed the next morning, having no suspicion that they owed their capture to the very women whose hospitality they had claimed." And Grace and Rachel found a messenger to carry the seized papers to General Greene, commander of the Continental Army in the South.

While some of Abram and Elizabeth's sons were wounded in the war, six survived. Grace's husband, William, was killed when he was aiming his cannon during the Siege of Augusta, after serving in the Sieges of Savannah and Charleston. Grace raised their two sons and a daughter on her own and never remarried. Rachel and Barkley Martin, who didn't have children, were reunited at war's end. Rachel lived into her 80s.

Grace and Rachel Martin are still remembered in South Carolina for their risky act.

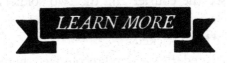

LEARN MORE

"Grace and Rachel Martin"
A Woman's Light: Making History in South Carolina
South Carolina State Museum
www.scmuseum.org/women/Martin.html

"The Martin Women of Edgefield 1851"
Women of South Carolina in the Revolution
http://sciway3.net/clark/revolutionarywar/womenof
revolution.html

Pioneer Mothers of America by Harry Clinton Green and Mary Clinton Green, Second Volume (G. P. Putnam's Sons, 1912)
https://archive.org

Women of the American Revolution, Vol. 1 by Elizabeth F. Ellet, contains a chapter on Grace and Rachel Martin
https://archive.org

Part Four

SOLDIERS AND DEFENDERS OF THE HOME FRONT

Elizabeth "Betty" Zane

◆◆◆

FLEET-FOOTED GIRL TO THE RESCUE

Sixteen-year-old Elizabeth "Betty" Zane ran, shots flying past her, one tearing her petticoat, until she escaped through the quickly opened and closed gate of Fort Henry. She was "a fair-haired, finely formed girl, athletic and active." Active and athletic were indeed what was needed that day at Virginia's Fort Henry (today in West Virginia). She had taken a chance, a life-threatening one.

On September 10, 1782, Ranger John Lynn had seen a group of Native Americans crossing the river in the vicinity of the fort. He knew that the young warriors of the Shawnee, Mingo, Delaware, Wyandot, and Miami tribes were allied with the British "in an effort to keep Americans from settling on their ancestral lands west of the Ohio River," says Greg Carroll, retired historian of the West Virginia Archives. He also knew that they could be a threat to the settlers who lived in or near the fort. The next day, Betty and some other settlers rushed into Fort Henry for protection.

Nancy Robbins and her mother were almost too late. They lived outside the fort and arrived just in time to squeeze past the strong wooden gate before it closed. Nancy's father wasn't so lucky. Trying to warn other settlers before he entered the fort, Indian warriors killed and scalped him and burned the family's cabin.

When the attack by the British and their Indian allies began, only about 20 men who lived in the settlement were inside the fort, along with about that many women and children, to fight off the company of 50 British, known as the Queen's Rangers, and 300 Native American attackers. Captain John Boggs, commander of Fort Henry, had left to find reinforcements. Betty's older brother, Colonel Silas Zane, along with two of her other older brothers, were in charge of the fort.

Only 25 homes, built of rough-hewn logs, made up the village of Wheeling, which edged Fort Henry. Betty's brothers—Ebenezer, Jonathan, and Silas—had established the village on the edge of the wilderness with the hopes of making it a permanent settlement.

For the previous 10 years, Betty, born July 19, 1765, in Moorefield, Virginia, the daughter of William Zane and Nancy Nolan, had been living very comfortably. She had been attending school in Philadelphia, a city of 20,000 people, of cobblestone streets, stores, and theatres.

At Fort Henry, along with other girls and women, Betty would have had a very different life. She would have spent her day making soap, spinning, weaving, or maintaining a fire (since it was a time before matches), living in a cabin built by her oldest brother, Colonel Ebenezer Zane. It was less than 100 yards from the fort and was built in response to attacks on the settlers by local Native Americans.

Colonel Ebenezer Zane didn't take shelter in the fort. He was in his cabin that day. His cabin wasn't an ordinary one but a blockhouse, a type of fort. There were small openings in

its walls that provided spaces to shoot through. Why the for-
tifications? A year earlier, during a previous attack on the fort
by the British and their Indian allies, Ebenezer and his family
had taken shelter in Fort Henry. While he was in the fort, his
cabin had been burned to the ground. After that, he rebuilt it,
increased its defense, and swore he would never leave it again.
For this attack, he had his own ammunition, and, like the settlers in the fort, was prepared for the attack.

And there was one, though not before the fort received a
demand for surrender by Britain's Captain Pratt. The settlers
didn't comply, and the fighting began. The walls of the wooden
fort were 17 feet high, with towers at each corner. Betty was in
the sentry box, a spot that had holes the settlers used to shoot
through with their rifles and muskets. From there she could
watch the attackers as she cooled and loaded guns for her brother
Jonathan. As bullets hit the walls around her, splitting off bits of
wood, she had to stop and pick splinters out of her arms.

On the morning of the second day of fighting, settlers inside
the fort realized they were low on gunpowder. Without it, they
wouldn't be able to continue to fight.

An abundance of ammunition was nearby, less than 100
yards away in Colonel Zane's cabin. Some in the fort suggested
that the man who could run the fastest should dash over and
bring back the needed powder. Some volunteered for the task.
It was a dangerous proposition, like volunteering to run across
a firing range.

Nancy Robbins, who had barely made it into the fort with
her mother, volunteered for the job, but she was very good at
molding the bullets that soldiers used in their muskets. The others wanted her to continue doing that.

Betty volunteered, too. And she had a persuasive argument:
she was a fast runner. Harry Green and Mary Wolcott Green,

in their book *The Pioneer Mothers of America*, imagined how the conversation might have gone:

> Several persons volunteered, among them being Elizabeth Zane. Her uncle, Silas Zane, refused.
> "Why not?" urged the girl. "I can go as well as not."
> "No," said Colonel Zane. "A man must go."
> "I can run as fast as any man," the girl persisted. "You have no man to spare. You need them all here, where I don't count."
> She was determined, fearless, young and impetuous, and she had her way.

Betty won the argument. As others opened the strong wooden gate on the east side, she ran out, attracting the attention of several Native Americans who watched. They didn't shoot but repeatedly shouted one word: *Squaw! Squaw! Squaw!*

Betty made it to the cabin unharmed. Inside, she told her brother what had happened. After tying a cloth around her waist to create a pouch, he emptied a keg of gunpowder into it. Clutching it to her, Betty ran out of his cabin and headed for Fort Henry. As she ran toward the fort, holding the pouch, the attackers must have realized she was aiding the fight. They started shooting as she ran, dodging bullets. One ripped through her petticoat, yet she ran unharmed into the opened door of the fort.

With the added ammunition, the siege continued that night, and by sunrise the next day the British and their Indian allies began a retreat, but not before burning cabins outside the fort and killing cattle. An hour later, Captain Boggs arrived with reinforcements. It was the last battle of the American Revolution. A victory, thanks to Betty's gunpowder run.

Four years later, Betty Zane married Ephraim McLaughlin. The two were eventually the parents of five daughters. Later

Betty Zane runs across the battle line carrying gunpowder.
Library of Congress LC-USZ62-2355

Ephraim died or disappeared. As the story goes, he went on a fishing trip down the Ohio River and was never seen again. Betty then married Jacob Clark. Along with many others in the Zane family, Betty and Jacob moved to Martins Ferry, Ohio, where they lived on land given to them by her brother Ebenezer. They had two children of their own. Betty lived in Martin's Ferry until her death on August 23, 1823.

A poem entitled "Elizabeth Zane" by John S. Adams included in the 1911 *Poems On Ohio* celebrated her feat:

> *This dauntless pioneer maiden's name*
> *Is inscribed in gold on the scroll of fame.*
> *She was the lassie who knew no fear*
> *When the tomahawk gleamed on the far frontier.*
> *If deeds of daring should win renown,*
> *Let us honor this damsel of Wheeling town,*
> *Who braved the savages with deep disdain,--*
> *Bright-eyed buxom Elizabeth Zane.*

BETTY OR MOLLY?

———— • ————

In 1849, 77 years after Betty Zane's "gunpowder run" and 26 years after her death, Lydia Boggs Shepherd Cruger, age 83, who was one of the last living eyewitnesses to the Siege of Fort Henry, claimed that it wasn't Betty who had made the gunpowder run. She claimed in a sworn statement that Molly Scott, another young woman who lived in the settlement, had done it.

During the siege, Molly was actually in Colonel Zane's cabin, not in the fort. Cruger also claimed that it was Colonel Zane and the men in the cabin who needed the gunpowder and that Molly ran from the cabin to the fort and back.

Who made the run? Molly Scott's grandson, James F. Scott, shared that he heard Molly herself tell "about the exploit of Betsy [sic] Zane carrying powder in her apron from Colonel Zane's dwelling to the fort, during the siege . . . as well as the narrow escape she had from the bullets of the Indians. . . . She [Scott] never gave any other name than Elizabeth or Betsy [sic] Zane, as he called her, as the one who carried the powder. She never claimed credit for herself." Letters and other documents support Scott's story and the story of Betty Zane's gunpowder run.

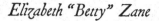

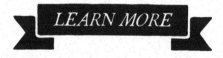

Betty Zane by Zane Grey (Charles Francis Press, 1903)
www.gutenberg.org/ebooks/1261

Betty Zane: Legend of Fort Henry
www.youtube.com/watch?v=Re23mR5YFH4

"Betty Zane, Lydia Boggs, and Molly Scott:
The Gunpowder Exploits at Fort Henry"
West Virginia Division of Culture and History
www.wvculture.org/history/journal_wvh/wvh55-4.html

"Elizabeth 'Betty' Zane"
West Virginia Division of Culture and History
www.wvculture.org/history/notewv/zane.html

Women of the American Revolution, Vol. II, by Elizabeth F. Ellet,
contains a chapter on Elizabeth Zane.
http://archive.org or Google Books

Deborah Sampson Gannett

UNDERCOVER SOLDIER

Deborah Sampson Gannett stood on a stage in Boston in March 1802 in front of a packed audience. Dressed in her military uniform—a jacket of deep blue, tight-fitting white pants, and a leather helmet topped with a bit of fur—and holding her musket in hand, she responded to shouted commands: "Poise—Firelock! . . . Take aim! Fire! Charge bayonet!"

The Boston audience went wild, as did the audiences in other cities in Massachusetts, Rhode Island, and New York during her one-year stage tour in 1802–03.

Deborah Sampson Gannett was acting out the role she played in real life as a soldier in the Continental Army. She had bound her breasts, dressed as a man, and signed up as Robert Shurtliff. She served for three years, living every day and night alongside her fellow soldiers. Why didn't anyone notice she was a woman?

Deborah Sampson was born just before Christmas on December 17, 1760, in Plympton, Massachusetts, one of six children. When she was only five, her father deserted the family. Deborah was sent to live with relatives since her mother was unable to

Deborah Sampson Gannett.
Library of Congress LC-USZ61-202

support all the children, and at age 10 she became an indentured servant in the Thomas family in nearby Middleborough. On their farm she milked cows, spread manure, and stacked bales of hay to earn the room and board offered by the family in exchange for her work.

Yet she also became part of the family. During winters, she often went to school along with the Thomas sons and learned to read and write. When, at age 18, in 1778, she completed her obligation to the Thomases and was free to begin a new life, she stayed with them and secured a teaching position at a nearby school.

Four years later, in the winter of 1781–82, when the Continental Congress put out a call for soldiers in the sixth year of the Revolution and few men volunteered, Deborah decided to do so. While visiting another family for a few days, she borrowed a suit of male clothing without telling her hosts, dressed herself as a man, visited the local recruiting office, and, on December 17, 1781, signed up using the name Timothy Thayer. She also took the offered cash payment for enlisting.

Perhaps elated with successfully signing up and beginning a new adventure, Deborah, still dressed as a man, stopped that evening in a local tavern. No one recognized her, and she had some drinks. According to a story related in *Masquerade: The Life and Times of Deborah Sampson* by Alfred F. Young, when it was time for the new recruits to report for duty, she didn't show up. Her absence was a topic of conversation at the recruiting office, which was in a private home. An older woman who had been in the home when Deborah signed the recruitment papers, who had known of Deborah when she was a schoolteacher in the area, commented that the young recruit had held a pen in the same way as Deborah Sampson. The woman voiced her suspicion that the recruit had been Deborah Sampson acting a part. Further inquiry led to the discovery of the borrowed suit of male clothing and of Deborah's attempt to enlist. When she was confronted, she returned the bounty she had been given— minus the money she had used to buy a new dress.

The following spring, Deborah decided to try again. Tying her long hair in a ponytail and binding her chest with cloth, she wore a man's suit and a ruffled shirt and traveled miles away from her home, away from people who might know her. On May 23, 1782, she signed up and became a private in the Fourth Massachusetts Regiment using the name Robert Shurtliff. Her first assignment was to a fort at West Point, one of the forts north of New York City, where she was chosen to be in the light infantry, the soldiers who marched before the main army. She was one of 10,000 soldiers who learned the formation drills she later performed onstage. She learned how to charge with a bayonet and load and shoot a musket twice in only a minute.

Fear of discovery must have been constantly on Deborah's mind. How did she manage to hide her identity? As explained by historian Sally Smith, "Deborah was about five feet eight inches tall. . . . Army shirts of the day were loose fitting and by binding her breasts, Deborah evidently managed to appear not significantly different from her fellow soldiers. The lack of a beard was not an obstacle, for the desperate continentals were enlisting teenage youth into the ranks."

But soldiers lived together, slept together, bathed together. When it came time for bed, like the other soldiers, Deborah shared a straw mattress with another soldier; yet, also like the other soldiers, she wore her uniform all day and all night as well.

There were close calls. On only her first assignment in June 1782, Deborah's unit traveled to White Plains, where they were ambushed. Among the reinforcements who showed up as backup, she saw the face of a neighbor of hers from home. Disguised, seen out of context, and given the tense situation, Deborah wasn't recognized by the neighbor.

She wasn't so lucky in the summer of 1782 in an area near Tarrytown. Deborah's unit was patrolling when it was attacked by a group of loyalists who charged with bayonets. While she fired with her musket, a loyalist soldier slashed her with a saber. Then she was shot in her leg. Her concerned sergeant carried Deborah on his horse to a French field hospital, where the doctor treating her first saw the head wound and treated it. When he asked her if she had other injuries, she denied it. Distracted by others who were injured, the doctor took her at her word and walked away.

Knowing the danger of her leg wound, however, Deborah picked up a silver surgical instrument she found nearby and used it to remove one musket ball from her thigh. A second musket ball was lodged too deep for her to pull it out and would remain in her leg for the rest of her life, causing her pain and discomfort. Deborah bandaged her leg, left the hospital, and made her way back to camp.

Deborah had enlisted late in the war. The English had actually surrendered at Yorktown, Virginia, in October 1781, months before Deborah enlisted, but she and the others were recruited to handle conflicts that continued during the peace negotiations. Those were the conflicts in which she and her fellow soldiers fought against loyalist groups that led attacks on civilians and soldiers loyal to America.

While it seemed as though the war would end before Deborah would be discovered, her luck finally ran out. While camped with her unit in Philadelphia, she contracted a fever that affected many in the camp. When she was taken to the hospital, she was too sick to be cautious and was probably asleep when a Dr. Barnabas Binney examined her and discovered her secret. Instead of turning her in, he took her to his home so that she could recuperate, and he encouraged her to continue in her identity as Robert Shurtliff.

While Dr. Binney kept Deborah's secret even from his family, he did reveal it to someone who mattered: General John Paterson, the commander of West Point. When Deborah later met with General Paterson, she admitted her true identity. Instead of retaliating, however, he treated her with kindness. That meeting took place six weeks after the signing of the treaty that officially ended the war. Robert Shurtliff was honorably discharged from the army on October 25, 1783, and Deborah Sampson began a new chapter of her life.

By 1792, almost 10 years later, she had married Benjamin Gannett and given birth to three children. In postwar America, making ends meet was a challenge. Like many other soldiers before her, she sent a petition to the Commonwealth of Massachusetts to claim the money she was owed from her time as a soldier. While she waited more than a decade for her claim to be approved, Deborah was creative and resourceful. Realizing she had quite a story to tell, she worked with a local writer, Herman

Mann, to write *The Female Review,* a book about her life, as well as a theatrical piece about her time as a solider. In 1802–03 she went on the road in a show titled *Mrs. Gannett's (Late Deborah Sampson) "The American Heroine."* Handbills promoting her show were passed out in the towns where she performed. It was the first lecture tour by an American woman.

It wasn't that Deborah wanted fame, though perhaps she enjoyed it. She needed money to support her family. While she received a small pension from the state of Massachusetts and made some profit from speaking engagements, it was not enough to end her worries. Moved by Deborah's impoverished situation, Boston's Paul Revere helped with her appeal for an additional pension from the government by writing a letter on her behalf, dated February 20, 1804. He ended his letter with the words: "I have no doubt your humanity will prompt you to do all in Your power to get her some relief, I think her case much more deserving than hundreds to whom Congress have been generous." The result was an additional pension for Deborah.

While Deborah first appeared onstage dressed as a woman, by the end of the performance she was dressed in her military uniform. She marched, performed drills with her musket, and told audiences details of her life as Robert Shurtliff. But she didn't reveal *too* many of the gritty details. "Thus I became an actor in that important drama," she said to her audiences. She asked them to imagine "the perils and inconvenience of a girl in her teens."

As she ended her Boston performance as Robert Shurtliff, soldier with the Continental Army, Deborah Sampson Gannett roused the audience by singing "God Save the Sixteen States."

LETTER OF PAUL REVERE ON BEHALF OF DEBORAH SAMPSON GANNETT

———— • ————

Mrs. Deborah Gannet of Sharon informes me, that she has inclosed to Your Care a petition to Congress in favour of Her. My works for Manufacturing of Copper, being at Canton, but a short distance from the Neighborhood where she lives: I have been induced to enquire her situation, and Character, since she quitted the Male habit, and Soldiers uniform; for the more decent apparrel of her own Sex; & Since she has been married and become a Mother. —— Humanity, & Justice, obliges me to say, that every person with whom I have conversed about Her, and it is not a few, speak of Her as a woman of handsom talents, good Morals, a dutifull Wife and an affectionate parent. ——She is now much out of health; She has several Children; her Husband is a good sort of a Man, 'tho of small force in business; they have a few acres of poor land which they cultivate, but they are really poor.

She told me, she had no doubt that her ill health is in consequence of her being exposed when She did a Soldiers duty; and that while in the Army, She was wounded. We commonly form our Idea of the person whom we hear spoken off, whom we have never seen; according as their actions are described, when I heard her spoken off as a Soldier, I formed the Idea of a tall, Masculine female, who had a small share of understandg, without education, & one of the meanest of her Sex. — When I saw and discoursed with I was agreeably supprised to find a small, effeminate, and converseable Woman, whose education entitled her to a better situation in life.

I have no doubt your humanity will prompt you to do all in Your power to get her some relief, I think her case much more deserving than hundreds to whom Congress have been generous.

I am Sir with esteem & respect Your humble Servant

Paul Revere

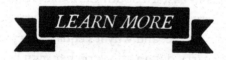

LEARN MORE

"Letter on Behalf of Deborah Sampson Gannett"
The Paul Revere House
www.paulreverehouse.org/gift2/details/46-51.pdf

Masquerade: The Life and Times of Deborah Sampson, Continental Soldier by Alfred Young (Alfred A. Knopf, 2004)

Women of the American Revolution by Mary R. Furbee (Lucent Books, 1999)

Rebecca Motte

A STRAIGHT-ARROW HEROINE

Rebecca Motte had a regal presence and appearance and was a member of one of the wealthiest and most prominent families of Charleston, South Carolina, as well as the mistress of several large plantations in eastern South Carolina. That's why at least one of seven dirty, scruffy prisoners was surprised when she engineered their escape, and why it's equally surprising that she helped a militia carry out an attack on her own home.

While serving in the Continental Army in South Carolina, Daniel Green had been captured on May 12, 1780, and confined to a prison ship, where he worked as a boat hand and was able to leave the ship to retrieve fresh water and supplies on land. On one such mission in March 1781, only two guards oversaw Green and six other prisoners. When Green and the other prisoners realized they could overpower the guards, they did so and then ran. Eventually Daniel Green and the other men ended up at Rebecca Motte's plantation.

Rebecca cautioned the fugitives to hide during the day and sent food to them on the sly, since they were in danger of being

Rebecca Motte.
The Pictorial Field-Book of the Revolution *by Benson J. Lossing, 1860*

recaptured. Then she planned their escape to a safer area in conjunction with the departure of a young lady who had been visiting her.

That night one of her servants led the escapees to the river, where they were ferried across in canoes. Then the servant led them up to the waiting overseer's house for food and drink. Beds and bedclothes were provided for them. The men slept near the fire and in the morning were told to take what provisions they would need for their trip. Daniel Green later wrote:

> [To think] of one so accomplished showing so much kindness and attention to us, of late so unused to humane treatment! . . . we were ragged, dirty, rough-looking fellows; yet notwithstanding our forlorn condition, they treated us as equals, spoke to us kindly, and made us feel that we had not served our country in vain.

Elegant ladies had to be gutsy during the Revolution. Rebecca Motte was gutsy more than once.

Rebecca Brewton was born on June 28, 1738. Before the Revolution, her Charleston family was among the wealthiest in South Carolina. In her early 20s, Rebecca married Jacob Motte, a wealthy plantation owner who served in the provincial legislature. They were the parents of six children, though only three of them lived to be adults. The fathers of both Rebecca and Jacob were the principal merchant bankers of mid-century South Carolina. Rebecca's older brother, Miles Brewton, owned several ships and numerous plantations, and he was elected to the second Provincial Congress, a position of prestige. But in

1775, while he and his entire family were on their way to Philadelphia by ship, they died when they were lost at sea.

After Miles's death, Rebecca and her three daughters lived in Miles Brewton's house, a brick townhouse in Charleston that is today a national historic landmark. When the British took over Charleston on May 12, 1780, officers seized the house and confined Rebecca and her family to a few rooms. It required control on her part to live side by side with officers of the occupying British Army. After her husband died of his illness in January 1780, she decided to move with her daughters and her nephew's widow, Mary Weyman Brewton, to Mt. Joseph, one of the family's plantations. They traveled there by horseback over forested hills, and by swamplands to the home, which overlooked the Congaree River.

Mrs. Motte's home was fortified and turned into Fort Motte.
The Pictorial Field-Book of the Revolution *by Benson J. Lossing, 1860*

In May 1781 Rebecca was living in the house on that same South Carolina plantation when 65 British soldiers, under the command of Captain Donald McPherson, arrived and took over. Once again Rebecca found herself and her family limited to a few rooms of their own home.

The soldiers dug a trench around the house, constructed a wall to surround it, and turned it into what they called Fort Motte. From its position on top of a hill just above the Congaree River, the British could spot any boats bringing supplies along the river going to and from Charleston, the main city in South Carolina. If the British had control of the river and the flow of supplies, they could retain control of the area. Fort Motte was one of a strategically located string of forts throughout the state. Control of the forts meant control of South Carolina. That was the British goal.

Meanwhile, the local militia, bent on foiling British plans and on reclaiming South Carolina for the Revolution, had the same goal. Leading the effort was Francis Marion—nicknamed "the Swamp Fox" because he and his men avoided the enemy by hiding out in swamps, and Henry "Light Horse Harry" Lee, known for his ability to ride a horse. With their militia, Marion and Lee approached the Motte plantation with the intent of dislodging the British from the fort. And they had to be clever in their approach.

After Captain McPherson saw the militia arrive, he ordered Rebecca and her family out. As they were leaving, carrying what they could, to move to a simple wooden farmhouse on an opposite hill but still on the plantation, Mary Weyman Brewton hesitated and picked up a quiver of arrows that had belonged to Rebecca's brother, ones he'd reputedly gotten from a military man involved in the East India trade. She mentioned to Rebecca that the arrows would be safer in her care. Later, those arrows would come in handy.

As the militia readied its attack on the fort, Henry Lee set up on the hill near the farmhouse where Rebecca and her family were staying. Francis Marion and his troops positioned themselves on another side. The ditch around the fort made it logistically difficult for his troops to get close enough to attack, yet they set up a six-pounder (a cannon) and began using it to pound the walls of the fort.

Inside Fort Motte, Captain McPherson and his troops weren't faring too well either. They didn't have any heavy artillery—cannons or other large guns—and were running out of ammunition. They needed backup.

It was almost there. Captain McPherson could see the campfires of the British Lord Rawdon and his troops, who were camped across the river on a hill. Marion, Lee, and Rebecca could see their campfires as well and realized that by the next day, Rawdon's troops would join McPherson's, and Marion and Lee wouldn't be able to defeat them. They had to take action before Rawdon's troops arrived. Rebecca likely watched Marion's troops continue to fire at the walls of the fort, but the shots weren't having a strong effect.

Rebecca listened as Marion and Lee plotted, then she interrupted, telling them that her house occupied almost all of Fort Motte. Her comment gave Lee and Marion an idea that they didn't want to suggest. If they set fire to her house, the British would have to run out of it and surrender.

Yet it seemed too drastic a measure. It was the elegant Mrs. Motte's home. She had been a gracious hostess and had also been nursing the sick and wounded that were in their company.

But when they told her their idea, she not only embraced it, but retrieved the arrows her cousin had taken from the house and presented them to Marion as the means of shooting fire at the house.

Rebecca Motte giving her arrows to Francis Marion.
United States Senate

The plan was accepted and put in place. In the morning Rebecca, her daughters, her niece, Marion, Lee, and their militia waited and watched as the sun rose and its rays beat down on the shingles of the roof of Rebecca's house. The hotter the shingles were, the quicker they would catch fire. Lord Rawdon and his men had not yet arrived. By noon on May 12, 1781, Marion and his men crept close enough to the fort to shoot at it with an arrow.

Prior to implementing their plan, however, they gave Captain McPherson warning of their attack, a not-uncommon practice that gave the opposing side a chance to evaluate the situation and choose to fight or surrender. Lord Rawdon and his troops hadn't arrived and wouldn't before Marion and Lee's plan was put into effect. A surrender would save lives. McPherson declined the offer.

The attack began. Some arrows were fired via rifles, but not all. Rebecca and the others watched as, according to an 1846 account, a

> bow was put into the hands of Nathan Savage, a private in Marion's brigade. . . . Balls of blazing rosin and brimstone were attached to the arrows, and . . . sent by the vigorous arm of the militia-man against the roof. They took effect, in three different quarters, and the shingles were soon in a blaze. McPherson immediately ordered a party to the roof, but this had been prepared for, and the fire of the six-pounder soon drove the soldiers down. The flames began to rage, the besiegers were on the alert, guarding every passage, and no longer hopeful of Rawdon, McPherson hung out the white flag imploring mercy.

After the surrender, the British soldiers joined the militia-men in putting out the fire—basically saving Rebecca's home. It wasn't just a kind gesture; they were likely afraid the flames would ignite the gunpowder stored in the house. Instead of being taken as prisoners, the British soldiers were paroled: they agreed they wouldn't again fight against the Revolution.

What happened next might be hard to believe. Rebecca provided a lavish dinner for both the British and the American officers, using the social gathering to dampen the hostility of the afternoon's events.

After the siege of Fort Motte and other conflicts that finally ended the war, Rebecca was saddled with the debts of her dead husband. Like many others, she had lost all of her property, with the exception of her slaves. Vowing to pay off her debts and regain her financial independence, she appealed to a friend to loan her the money to buy land on the Santee River on which she could grow rice. She had slave quarters and a simple home built for herself, and she concentrated on making the new plantation a success. By 1806 she was recovering financially and wrote to one of her children:

> Now I have told you all the news I know of, I will inform you about my crop. I have a better prospect of a good crop than I have ever had; there were more pains taken in planting; all my seed-rice was hand-picked; and if rice should be a good price next year, I shall pay all my debts, I hope . . .
> Your affectionate mother,
>
> R. Motte

Rebecca continued to live at her plantation on the Santee River and was seen around the area, according to *A Charleston Album* by Margaret Hayne Harrison, wearing "a high crowned ruffled mobcap, a square white neck kerchief pinned down in front, tight elbow sleeves, black silk mittens on her hands and arms and a full skirt with a pocket, a silver chain from which hung a pincushion, scissors and keys."

She died on January 10, 1815, at the age of 76.

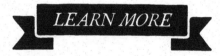

LEARN MORE

A Charleston Album by Margaret Hayne Harrison
(R. R. Smith, 1953)
Available on Google Books

The Pictorial Field-Book of the Revolution by Benson J. Lossing
(Harper Brothers, 1860)

"Mrs. Motte Directing Generals Marion and Lee to
Burn Her Mansion to Dislodge the British"
United States Senate
www.senate.gov/artandhistory/art/artifact/Painting
_33_00001.htm

Women of the American Revolution, Vol. II by Elizabeth F. Ellet,
contains a chapter on Rebecca Motte.
https://archive.org

Martha Bratton

"IT WAS I WHO DID IT"

On the day that Martha Bratton was in the field harvesting wheat on her South Carolina plantation, British captain Christian Huck and just more than 100 soldiers—some British Legion dragoons or cavalry, dozens of loyalist militia, and other mounted infantry—set out to capture Martha's husband, Colonel William Bratton, and their neighbor Captain John McClure, who were both leaders of the local patriot militia. It was July 11, 1780.

South Carolina was under British control. In May 1780 General Benjamin Lincoln, who was in charge of the Continental Army in South Carolina, had been taken prisoner along with his army. Opposition to the British had stopped. Most people in support of the Revolution thought the situation was hopeless. Yet some, like Martha's husband and McClure, didn't think so. They organized the local militia to fight back.

Captain Huck and his troops stopped first at the McClure home but got there too late. Captain McClure had already rejoined the main militia forces. That didn't stop Huck. McClure's younger brother, James, and the McClures' brother-

154

in-law Edward "Ned" Martin were there. When Huck discovered they had been melting pewter dishes and using the metal to mold bullets to be used by the militia, he ordered that the men be taken prisoner and hung the next morning. To punish the McClures's mother, he set fire to her home.

Once Huck and his men left, the McClures's mother quickly put out the fire and sent her daughter, Mary, to the militia camp to alert her son and Martha's husband, Colonel Bratton. Martha, wearing an ankle-length dress and a ruffled white cap on her head, was with her children on the front porch as the British approached. Soldiers led by Lieutenant William Adamson arrived first and told her they were looking for her husband. She replied that she didn't know where he was.

At that, a soldier named Henry lost his temper and grabbed a reaping hook—a curved blade used for harvesting grain—that was hanging on the porch wall. Holding Martha from behind, he placed the hook at her throat and threatened to behead her if she didn't reveal her husband's whereabouts. Martha's son William, then age six, watched, horrified.

Then, Lieutenant Adamson stepped in. He struck Henry with a sword, then beat and kicked him as Martha and William watched. Adamson then apologized for Henry's threat.

Martha accepted the apology and went into her home. Captain Huck and his dragoons then arrived. Entering her house, Huck repeated the question Adamson had asked: "Where is your husband?"

"He is in Sumter's army," Martha said defiantly, referring to General Thomas Sumter, who was one of the leaders of the South Carolina militia during the American Revolution.

Then Huck turned on the charm. He took William on his knee, treating him kindly. Martha's other children—Elisa, 13, Jane, 11, and Martha, 9—stood watching as Captain Huck tried

A 19th-century romanticized version of Martha Bratton being threatened with a reaping hook.
The Story of a Great Nation, 1888; courtesy of Historical Center of York County, Culture and Heritage Museums

to persuade Martha that her husband should join the British side.

Martha was firm, stating that she'd rather he was loyal to his country even if he was to die fighting for it.

On hearing that, Huck stood up abruptly and pushed William off his knee with such force that the boy fell on the floor and broke his nose, but Martha still refused to share any information.

Captain Huck, surely angry with her, demanded that Martha cook dinner for them. As she did, Huck taunted her with the news that he planned to order her house burned the next day.

After supper and before departing, Huck ordered that Martha and her children be locked in the upstairs room to ensure Martha wouldn't have the opportunity to alert her husband.

Taking his troops to an adjacent farm that conveniently had a field of oats that his horses could snack on, a home he could sleep in, and fields for his men to sleep on, Captain Huck and his troops settled in for the night.

Meanwhile, William Bratton and other militia were on their way. Bratton might have wondered about the chances of approximately 130 Whig militia defeating Huck's better-trained force. Yet when he discovered where Huck and his men were camped, he realized his advantage: he knew the area. He ordered some of the men to block the two main escape routes. In the darkness, his men positioned themselves behind trees and fences and waited for dawn. It was the kind of guerilla warfare tactic so often employed in the South during the American Revolution.

Soon after Captain Huck's troops rose and began eating breakfast, they realized they were surrounded and cut off from easy escape. Some got away by running to the woods. Others tried to fight. Captain Huck mounted his horse and, waving his sword above his head, attempted to rally his troops, but he was shot and killed.

With Huck dead, Lieutenant William Adamson—the one who had saved Martha's life—vainly attempted to inspire the troops to keep fighting. Then, as he tried to get his horse to jump over a ditch, he fell off of his horse onto branches that pierced his chest. He lay bleeding, seriously wounded.

The British troops faltered and retreated to the area of the Bratton home with the patriot militiamen in pursuit. When some of the bullets hit the Bratton home, Martha sheltered her younger children in the fireplace, but the battle was over soon.

Surprisingly, the militia forces were victorious in a battle that had taken less than a half hour.

Yet William Bratton wasn't finished. He had heard the story of Martha being threatened with a reaping hook. He incorrectly thought it was Adamson—the one who had saved her life—who had done it. He searched for him, found him wounded and bleeding, and accused him. "I beg of you to consult Mrs. Bratton before you perpetrate so great a wrong," said Adamson in return.

As Martha made her way to join them, she could have seen the many wounded and dead soldiers lying about the field along with the tools of war—saddles, bridles, pistols, swords—that had been cast aside during the battle. When she approached, Colonel Bratton didn't waste time in presenting her to Adamson, who said, "Madam, you were sent for at my request . . . more to save your husband from a cruel injustice to himself than for any service you may be able to render me. He has heard it was I who threatened your life."

Once Colonel Bratton realized his error, he gave Adamson some rum to ease his pain and saw that he was carried to the Bratton home. Young William later wrote in his memoir, "My Mother, who was skilled in concocting salves and poultices, dressed his wound and he was made as comfortable as circumstances would permit."

As the sun was coming up, other wounded men from both sides were also taken to Martha's house, and some of Martha's neighbors—local women—came by to help minister to them. Patriot soldiers took the dead outside. But even though Martha was on the patriot side, when she watched two patriots pick up a dead British soldier with one holding his head and the other his feet and throw him out of the house, she reprimanded them for their callousness. They, in return, "laughed at my Mother," William wrote later.

HARVESTING THE CROPS

—————— • ——————

As more and more South Carolina men joined the militia and left their farms behind, wives, other women, and older men took up the task of caring for the crops. One woman, Mary Gill Mills (1758–1841), who was born in Pennsylvania but moved to South Carolina, in 1780 was "one of a band of eleven women who went from farm to farm to reap the crops for the fighting men in the army."

This short conflict, later called the Battle of Huck's Defeat, was an important victory. It showed that a smaller militia force led by militiamen like Colonels Bratton and McClure could defeat the British cavalry. That boosted the morale and support of the rebels in South Carolina. More joined the militia ranks to continue the fight. And women like Mrs. McClure and Martha Bratton continued to play a part.

After the Battle of Huck's Defeat, the war in South Carolina was far from over. Wives like Martha Bratton, grandmothers and grandfathers, young women, and even children often had to defend their homes and themselves while husbands, fathers, and young men were away fighting.

To help the residents against random attacks by British soldiers or Tories, South Carolina's pro-Revolution governor, John Rutledge, sent supplies of gunpowder to each of the local militia regiments to be distributed to families. Once families received it, they hid it—sometimes in trees, in buildings, anywhere it wouldn't be easily found.

"It's important to note," says historian Michael Scoggins, "that while people could make bullets by melting down pewter dishes, gunpowder had to be made in a factory, which had to be either up north or in Britain."

That meant that gunpowder, which was crucial for those in the neighborhoods in South Carolina where the Brattons and other families lived, was hard to get. Without it, neither the families nor the militia could defend themselves.

Sometime after the Battle of Huck's Defeat, Martha Bratton was at home when one of her neighbors warned her that a British officer had sent a group of his soldiers to seize the gunpowder hidden on her farm. Hearing this, Martha grabbed a pistol, jumped on her horse, and headed off to where a barrel of powder was hidden in an oak tree.

When she got to the tree, Martha removed the barrel, pulled off the lid, and began creating a trail of gunpowder from the oak to the middle of the road upon which the British were approaching. As they came closer, she aimed her pistol at the trail of powder and fired, igniting the gunpowder. When the spark reached the barrel, and as the British watched, the supply of gunpowder exploded.

The British soldier in charge was furious. He demanded to know who was responsible.

"It was I who did it," Martha replied. "Let the consequence be what it will, I glory in having prevented the mischief contemplated by the cruel enemies of my country."

Martha was put under house arrest and told not to leave her house, even to attend church, for 30 days. If she didn't comply, she was threatened with further punishment.

If the Battle of Huck's Defeat gave new hope to the patriots, actions like Martha's destruction of the gunpowder boosted their effort and morale. Patriot forces were eventually victorious in South Carolina.

After the war, Colonel Bratton returned to his plantation and to the home he had built for his family. He and Martha continued farming and operated a tavern in their home—with a room for those who needed a place to stay—in the 1780s and '90s. Colonel Bratton was also justice of the peace, a judge, and a member of the South Carolina House and Senate. Martha died in 1816, a few months after William, who died in 1815.

BRATTONSVILLE

———•———

Today the home of Martha and William Bratton is part of Historic Brattonsville, a 775-acre living-history village and Revolutionary War battlefield site listed on the National Register of Historic Places. The village of Brattonsville was named for the Bratton family. Martha and William's son, John, inherited the Bratton home. He and his wife, Harriet, later added a wing and the house became the Brattonsville Female Seminary, a school for girls. Visitors can explore more than 30 historic structures, see reenactments of the Battle of Huck's Defeat, see the porch where Martha was threatened with the reaping hook or the area where the gunpowder incident took place, or see demonstrations of farming techniques from the Revolutionary era through the 1840s.

The Day It Rained Militia: Huck's Defeat and the Revolution in the South Carolina Backcountry May–July 1780 by Michael Scoggins (The History Press, 2005)

Fearless Martha: A Daughter of the American Revolution by Sheila Ingle (Hub City Press, 2011)

"**Historic Brattonsville**"
Culture and Heritage Museums
http://chmuseums.org/brattonsville

Women of the American Revolution, Vol. I, by Elizabeth F. Ellet, contains a chapter on Martha Bratton
https://archive.org

Part Five

LEGENDARY LADIES

Molly Pitcher

◆◆◆

"POSSIBLE MOLLIES" MARY LUDWIG HAYES AND MARGARET COCHRAN CORBIN

It was over 100 degrees on June 28, 1778, at the Battle of Monmouth. Many men died of heatstroke. Many women were on the New Jersey battlefield that day as well, carrying water to thirsty soldiers, nursing the wounded, and sponging cannons with water to cool them. One woman was helping her husband as he operated a cannon when he was shot. What did she do?

Dr. Albigence Waldo, a surgeon, heard of her actions from an officer he treated. Five days later, the doctor wrote in his journal:

> One of the camp women I must give a little praise to. Her gallant [husband], whom she attended in battle, being shot down, she immediately took up his gun and cartridges and like a Spartan heroine fought with astonishing bravery, discharging the piece with as much regularity as any soldier present. This a wounded officer,

whom I dressed, told me he did see himself, she being in his platoon, and assured me I might depend on its truth.

A woman taking over a cannon would have been quite a sight to see. Perhaps, though, she wasn't the only woman helping with a cannon that day.

Seventeen-year-old Continental Army private Joseph Plumb Martin wrote of what he saw that day, though his saucy description that was included in his diary wasn't printed until 50 years later, in 1830:

A woman whose husband belonged to the artillery and who was then attached to a piece in the engagement, attended with her husband at the piece for the whole time.

While in the act of reaching a cartridge and having one of her feet as far before the other as she could step, a cannon shot from the enemy passed directly between her legs without doing any other damage than carrying away all the lower part of her petticoat.

Looking at it with apparent unconcern, she observed that it was lucky it did not pass a little higher, for in that case it might have carried away something else. . . .

But who was she? Neither entry mentions her name. Were the men speaking of the same woman?

Ten years after the appearance of Martin's diary account, George Washington Parke Custis, the grandson of Martha Washington and the step-grandson of George Washington, sketched and described his version of the scene that took place at the Battle of Monmouth:

While Captain Molly was serving some water for the refreshment of the men, her husband received a shot in the head, and fell lifeless under the wheels of the piece. The heroine threw down the pail of water, and crying to her dead consort, "Lie there my darling while I avenge ye," grasped the ramrod, . . . sent home the charge, and called to the matrosses to prime and fire. It was done. Then entering the sponge into the smoking muzzle of the cannon, the heroine performed to admiration the duties of the most expert artillerymen, while loud shots from the soldiers rang along the line. . . .

The next morning . . . Washington received her graciously, gave her a piece of gold and assured her that her services should not be forgotten. This remarkable

George Washington salutes Captain Molly on the field at Monmouth.
Drawing by George Washington Parke Custis, The Pictorial Field-Book of the Revolution *by Benson J. Lossing, 1860*

and intrepid woman survived the Revolution, never for an instant laying aside the appellation she has so nobly won . . . the famed Captain Molly at the Battle of Monmouth.

Custis gave her a name: Captain Molly. Custis's story and sketch appeared in the *National Intelligencer* on February 22, 1840, and later in his book, *Recollections and Private Memoirs of Washington*, in 1860. A friend of his, author-illustrator Benson Lossing, was taken with the tale, and with permission included Custis's sketch and story in his book *The Pictorial Field-Book of the Revolution* in 1860. Molly's fame spread. Yet who was she?

In 1848 artists Nathaniel Currier and his partner James Merritt Ives, also taken with the story, painted the scene, depicting her as strong and resolute. They called the painting *The Heroine of Monmouth, Molly Pitcher,* giving her another name. It stuck. Other artists drew her and called her that as well. They spread her fame.

Why Molly Pitcher? Many women on the battlefields of the American Revolution carried water to either cool the cannons or to quench the thirst of the soldiers. Did they carry the water in pails or pitchers? Pails make more sense. Yet one writer suggested how the name may have come about. "Thirsty, weary soldiers calling out, 'Water! Over here, Molly! Bring that pitcher over here!' And, finally, 'Molly! Pitcher!'" That was one guess. Whether it evolved that way or another way, the name stuck.

Almost 30 years later, Currier & Ives again depicted "Molly Pitcher," this time presenting a slimmer, more lithe Molly and describing her as "The wife of a Gunner in the American Army" who when her husband was killed took his place at the gun, and served throughout the battle." Yet another artist, Edward Percy Moran, depicted a rather dressed-up Molly taking a more casual stance.

Painting by Currier & Ives.
Library of Congress LC-USZC2-3186

Molly Pitcher's image was also used in images to sell cartridges and many other items. She was celebrated on a 1928 US postage stamp. During World War II the Liberty ship SS *Molly Pitcher* was launched. A stretch of US Route 11 in Pennsylvania is known as the Molly Pitcher Highway.

Painting by Edward Percy Moran.
Library of Congress LC-USZC4-4969

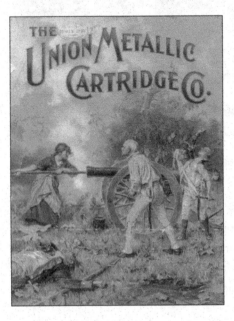

Advertisement for the Union Metallic Cartridge Co. by artist Gilbert Gaul.
Library of Congress LC-USZC2-51103

However, Molly Pitcher is a name given to an image of a woman depicted by artists who represented the courage and fortitude of American women on the battlefield during the American Revolution, it is not the name of a real person. Molly Pitcher's fame was spread by the many images of her painted by artists over the years.

Did anyone find out who the actual woman was who took over the cannon for her husband that day at Monmouth? People wanted to know. For years, many books claimed she was red-haired Mary Hays. What the various artists may or may not have known was that Mary Hays was described in her time as "homely in appearance with an eye defect; not refined in manner or language; of average height and heavy set . . . a great talker; smoked and chewed tobacco."

That was not the image artists drew. It was probably an accurate description of her, though, and likely of some of the other women who traveled with their soldier husbands during the American Revolution. They were called camp followers, women who followed their husbands to war—some with children in tow—because they had no way of supporting themselves at home or were afraid of punishment by Tories, or of British soldiers who raided and ransacked many homes.

Mary Ludwig Hays may have been one of these camp followers. Like other camp followers, Mary may have helped carry water to men at the Battle of Monmouth, but historians now doubt whether she was even there. That's just one of the questions about her. Historians are also not sure of the identity of her husband. She could have been married to William Hays or John Casper Hays, but according to several sources, when her husband—William or John—enlisted in the Continental Army, she went along with him. The sketchy and conflicting details available about her life reflect the lack of historical record of many

CAMP FOLLOWERS

———————— • ————————

Many wives accompanied their husbands to war as did Mary Hays and Margaret Corbin. One such camp follower was 32-year-old Maria Cronkite. When her husband, a musician in the First New York Regiment, joined the army in 1777, she followed him, and during his enlistment she gave birth to several children and cared for them while she worked as a washerwoman for officers until the end of the war.

Camp followers helped out by washing clothes, as did Maria, or cooking, and sometimes they performed unpleasant tasks. At the Battle of Bemis Heights in upstate New York in October 1777, women made trips during the night to take clothes off of the dead and also to retrieve valuables or weapons.

One camp follower, Sarah Osborn, was married to Aaron Osborn, a blacksmith and Revolutionary War veteran in 1780. He didn't tell her when he reenlisted, but he wanted her to go with him. At first she refused, but she agreed after his superior, Captain James Gregg, told her that "she should have the means of conveyance either in a wagon or on horseback." That was important to her. According to orders from George Washington, the camp-following women were not to ride in the wagons but to walk behind the troops as they traveled. That winter Sarah instead rode in wagons and sleighs while many other women camp followers walked with the troops as they traveled hundreds of miles north and south. She earned her keep by washing and sewing for soldiers and on one occasion by baking bread.

While soldiers were busy building trenches and sheltering themselves from gunfire, Sarah brought beef, bread, and coffee to them. On one of these trips, she met General George Washington, who asked her if she "was not afraid of the cannonballs?" Her answer: "It would not do for the men to fight and starve too."

There was yet another camp follower who was concerned about the men and personally about George Washington. Since the commander in chief of the Continental Army was away from his home for six years during the war, his wife and confidante, Martha, traveled by carriage to be with him at the army's winter quarters when fighting was suspended. She was his secretary and acted as an intermediary between her husband and those seeking his assistance, boosted morale when she comforted sick or wounded soldiers, and hosted social events for officers and their wives, political leaders, and visiting foreign dignitaries.

ordinary men and women of the Revolutionary era whose lives were not set down in history books.

After her husband died a few years after the war, Mary married George McCauley, becoming Mary McCauley. She worked at the ordinary job of cleaning and scrubbing buildings. More than 40 years after her actions on Monmouth, she was recognized by the Pennsylvania government for her service, not for her husband's, and was granted a small pension but was not identified as Molly Pitcher during her life. During the 1876 centennial in Cumberland County—well after her death on January 22, 1832—an elaborate tombstone was installed in her honor that included both her name and that of Molly Pitcher.

Margaret Cochran Corbin is another candidate who may have served as the inspiration for Molly Pitcher. However, Margaret wasn't at the Battle on Monmouth where the legend of Molly Pitcher began. When Margaret's husband, John Corbin, enlisted in the First Company of the Pennsylvania Artillery as a matross, one who loaded and fired cannons, she accompanied him and traveled with the troops as a camp follower. Margaret and John were at the New York Battle of Fort Washington in November 1776. While tending the cannon, John was killed by a shot to the head. His commander gave the order to pull the cannon out of the way. One author imagined the scene:

> Judge of his surprise when a wild-eyed and weeping young woman [Margaret], with hair flying, rushed up and besought him not to remove the gun. . . . "I know all about it," she said. "Jack has shown me. Let me fire it." He let her. And for several hours, she continued. Then, she was hit in the left shoulder. Others carried her away from the action.

The basic facts of this vivid story are true. John Corbin was killed and Margaret was wounded while manning a cannon, the scene so far depicted by artists.

Since Margaret Corbin was injured in the attack that killed her husband and was disabled by the shoulder wound, she appealed to the government for help and was the first woman to receive a pension from the United States. The resolution passed by the Continental Congress on July 6, 1779, reads:

> Resolved—That Margaret Corbin, wounded and disabled at the attack on Fort Washington, while she heroically filled the post of her husband, who was killed by her side serving a piece of artillery, do receive during her natural life, or continuance of said disability, one half the monthly pay drawn by a soldier in service of these States; and that she now receive out of public stores, one suit of clothes, or value thereof in money.

One suit of clothes! She actually got a new suit each year. An 87-year-old man who lived near her remembered seeing her and called her "the famous Irishwoman called Captain Molly . . . she generally dressed in the petticoats of her sex, with an artilleryman's coat over. Another local often saw her fishing in the Hudson River."

Margaret had a rough life. Born in Pennsylvania on November 12, 1751, she was just five or six when her father was killed and her mother was taken captive during a Native American raid. She never saw her mother again, and was raised by her uncle until she married John Corbin when she was 16 years old. A soldier's letter of September 15, 1785, from West Point, New York, site of an army fort, noted details of her later life: "I have procured a place for Capt. Molly till next spring, if she should live so long, about three miles from this place."

Over the next four years she "was also furnished with old bed-sacks (originally filled with straw and used as soldiers' mattresses), old sheets and even an old tent." She "was saluted as 'Captain Molly' til death ended her miseries."

When Margaret Corbin died around 1800, a cedar tree was planted at the head of her grave. In 1909 a monument to her was installed in her honor at Fort Tryon, New York, that was inscribed with the words: "Margaret Corbin—The first American woman to take a soldier's part in the War for Liberty." It was a tribute to her and not to the legendary Molly Pitcher.

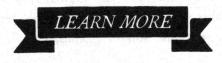

LEARN MORE

Founding Myths: Stories That Hide Our Patriotic Past by Ray Raphael (The New Press, 2004)

"Sarah Osborn Recollects Her Experiences in the Revolutionary War, 1837"
History Matters
http://historymatters.gmu.edu/d/5833

"Molly Pitcher: True or False?"
New Jersey History Game 2001
New Jersey's Monmouth County
www.co.monmouth.nj.us/page.aspx?Id=1729

Mammy Kate

❖❖❖

UNLIKELY RESCUER

Mammy Kate was concerned about Stephen Heard, a patriot militia officer. She was one of his slaves, and he had been sentenced to death.

But Heard cheated death. In 1894 Heard's great-granddaughter, Bevelle Comer Hampton—who was the wife of Robert Hampton—wrote down the story that has been shared in the family in what she called *A Family History*:

> The British captured Governor Heard and put him in prison in Augusta. Aunt Kate (a servant) heard of it and went to Augusta to see what she could do for him. She washed for the British officers and got them to let her take washing for the prisoners. In this way she saw Grand Papa & found that he was almost starving so she used to carry him a cake of corn bread concealed in her bosom every time she could get into the prison on any pretext.

> She [Aunt Kate] was a very large strong woman and Grand Papa was a small man so hearing one day that the British were going to shoot Grand Papa she took her basket and went into the prison as usual for the soiled clothes. Grand Papa got into the basket and the other prisoners packed the clothes around him and helped Aunt Kate put the basket on her head. She then walked boldly out and Grand Papa made good his escape. He offered Aunt Kate her freedom, but she refused to accept it.

Now *that's* a story worth remembering, and the family passed it on for generations.

Is it a legend—an unverified story handed down, passed along in families or communities—or is it true? If the story of Aunt Kate's rescue of Heard is even partially true, if she helped him escape in some way, Stephen Heard owed her his life. Who was she?

Few records exist of Mammy Kate's life. She was believed to have been from Africa, though no evidence exists of her birthplace. Public records establish that she was married to a man known as Daddy Jack, also one of Heard's slaves.

Many parts of the Mammy Kate story are a mystery. Stories abound and sometimes conflict. For example, how did she get to the fort, if she actually did? Did she walk? Did she go by horseback? Peggy Galis, a descendant of Stephen Heard, currently living in Georgia, still marvels at the feat. "The idea that Mammy Kate could find Augusta is so remarkable," says Galis. "She had to go more than 50 miles. Augusta was then the market center for that area and was where people went to sell deerskins or other things, so there's a chance she had been there, but it is still amazing that she got there at a time when slaves were purposely kept from knowing where they were so they didn't escape."

Yet was Heard even in Augusta? Many accounts state that Heard was captured while fighting in the Battle of Kettle Creek in February 1779, taken prisoner, and put in Augusta's Fort Cornwallis. But as historian Lee Ann Caldwell, director of the Center for the Study of Georgia History at Georgia Regents University, points out, "Augusta was not in British hands after the Battle of Kettle Creek; it had been re-occupied by the Patriots on the same day. Fort Cornwallis was not built until after Augusta was re-taken by the Loyalists over a year later in June 1780."

Then when was Heard captured? And where was he held? The fact that he was governor of Georgia from May 1780 to August 1781, during the Revolution, would have made him a prize catch.

And why would Mammy Kate have been nearby? "Perhaps Mammy Kate was a camp follower and traveled with the troops," says Lee Ann Caldwell. "Many wives or servants accompanied soldiers to war to provide services like washing or cooking. Perhaps she accompanied Stephen Heard as he traveled with the local militia. If so, she might have been in the area when he was captured. Most likely he was riding one of his own horses, Lightfoot or Silverheels, when captured, so his horse could have been there as well."

If she went, how many times did she visit?

One source, *Historical Collections of the Joseph Habersham Chapter, Daughters of the American Revolution, Volume II*, from 1902, suggests that she visited Heard often. It reads, "One of his faithful slaves would bring him food—usually an 'ash cake'— when she came for the prisoner's washing, to keep him from suffering hunger."

Another source, *The Official History of Elbert County, 1790–1935* by John H. McIntosh, suggests a single visit: "One morning, carrying on her head a large covered basket, she presented herself at the fort and asked the sentry on duty for the privilege of securing her master's soiled linen. The request was carelessly granted and the guard offered the information that, 'The damned Rebel would soon be hung.'"

McIntosh's and Mrs. Hampton's versions of how Mammy Kate helped Heard escape are very similar, with Kate sneaking him away inside a basket on her head. Mrs. Hampton's 1894 document doesn't say what happened next, but according to *Historical Collections of the Joseph Habersham Chapter, Daughters of the American Revolution, Volume II*, "She [Aunt Kate] managed to get his war horse 'Lightfoot,' from the enemy." Perhaps he'd been riding Lightfoot when he was captured and the horse was at the fort?

McIntosh gives a different explanation: "The night previous to this remarkable rescue she [Mammy Kate] brought two of Stephen Heard's fine Arabian horses, Lightfoot and Silverheels, to the outskirts of Augusta and left them in keeping of a trusted friend of her master."

As McIntosh tells it, after the escape:

While they were traveling homeward her master turned to her and said, "Kate, you have this day saved my life and I shall set you free."

"Na, Marse Stephen," she answered, "You may set me free, but I ain't gwiner set you free!"

After the Revolution, Stephen Heard acknowledged Mammy Kate when he received a land grant of more than 6,000 acres as payment for his military service. On the estate, which was set in a forest of trees, he built a home he called Heardmont and according to the Heard family descendants also provided Mammy Kate and her husband, Daddy Jack, with a small tract of land and a house on the estate. Was it to reward her for the rescue? Or was it for years of loyal service in the household? Lee Ann Caldwell explains, "Paternalistic owners often showed kindnesses to loyal house slaves. An example is when Mrs. Hampton referred to Kate as Aunt Kate in the family history. Terms such as Mammy, Aunt, or Uncle implied a special, favorable status."

That's a status that Mammy or Aunt Kate continues to hold. "When I was growing up I had the wonderful experience of having a woman who was a descendant of Mammy Kate care for me when my parents were at work," says Peggy Galis. "We used to talk about Mammy Kate a lot. She still remembered the house at Heardmont and she told us where Mammy Kate's cabin was."

Galis shares another story passed on through the family about another home on the property. "The house my grandmother and my father grew up in and I visited often was the one Stephen Heard built for his son, Thomas Jefferson Heard," says Galis. "Interestingly, every house that Heard built after the war had an escape route, a secret staircase, a way to get out to the river." Heard likely wanted a safe exit for his family in case of an attack, since the house was located on the edge of the area that was settled.

Did Mammy or Aunt Kate's cabin have an escape route? No records about that have surfaced, but another tidbit about Kate was passed on by Mrs. Hampton:

She [Aunt Kate] used to act as a spy for her master. She would go to the enemy's camp and eavesdrop there taking with her some little thing to sell as a pretext. Once she heard a Tory say—Stephen Heard must have dealings with the devil. He is obliged to have dealings with the devil else how could he always know what we are doing and what we are going to do. She said she could have told them all about that devil.

Perhaps Kate was also a spy.

After the war, Heard married a second time in 1785 to Elizabeth Darden of Virginia, beginning a new life. His first wife, Jane Germany, and their young adopted daughter (a child of Mrs. Heard's deceased sister) died during the Revolution as "the result of a cold caught one winter night while escaping from her home to a neighboring fort . . . for protection from Tories and Indians," wrote Mrs. Hampton in *A Family History*.

With his new wife, Elizabeth, Heard lived a long life. Together they had five sons and four daughters.

According to the family story, Mammy Kate and Daddy Jack also had nine children, and when Kate died she asked that each of Governor Heard's children be given one of her own.

When Heard died in November 1815 without a will, his son John Adams Heard, administrator of the estate, filed official papers with the court that listed all of Stephen Heard's property. Mammy Kate and Daddy Jack—noted as Jack and Cate—are listed as property.

"The story we always heard," says Peggy Galis, "is that Stephen Heard tried to grant her freedom but she didn't accept it. Instead he gave her the land and a place to live. It would have been dangerous for her. At some point she may have been re-enslaved. I try to imagine the loyalty that must have been involved."

One last sentence in Mrs. Hampton's document about Aunt Kate states, "When Aunt Kate died she requested that her remains be buried at the masters['] feet and if not there, she is buried near him."

Mammy Kate was indeed buried in the cemetery at Heardmont, where Stephen Heard was also buried. Her grave was marked with a marble headstone bearing her name.

Yet historians still doubt the truth of the Mammy Kate rescue. Did she really carry Heard out of the prison in a basket? Or did she aid his escape in another way? Documents and letters from a variety of sources could clarify the facts, but they've yet to be found, if they exist at all.

Others continue to honor Mammy Kate despite historians' doubts. On October 15, 2011, the Georgia Society Sons of the American Revolution (SAR) held a ceremony at the Heardmont

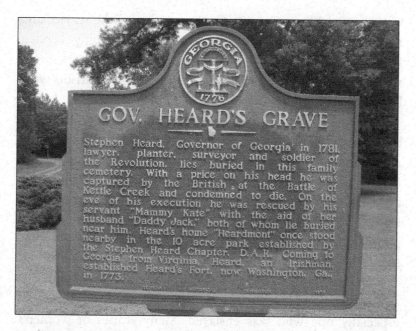

Stephen Heard's grave marker explains, he was rescued by his servant "Mammy Kate."
Courtesy of Michael Henderson, Lieutenant Commander, US Navy, Retired

The 2011 *Congressional Record* honors Mammy Kate.
United States Congress

Cemetery in Elbert County, Georgia, to honor the service and memory of Revolutionary patriots including not only Stephen Heard and four others but also Mammy Kate. Wreaths along with bronze SAR medallions proclaiming them as patriots were laid upon their gravestones.

Was Mammy Kate a patriot? During the Revolutionary War a patriot was a person who opposed the British and supported American independence. There were many ways of fighting the British, including spying or rescuing a prisoner. Some people are satisfied that Mammy Kate was a patriot. "She and anyone in his household would have automatically been considered a patriot since Heard, as head of the household was one," notes Lee Ann Caldwell.

Mammy Kate's story is an example of how hard it is to discover the facts of the life of a woman who lived 200 years ago, especially one who was enslaved. Many stories of women's experiences during the American Revolution were often not recorded in letters or documents. Some such records about Mammy Kate may yet be discovered.

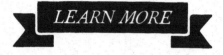

LEARN MORE

"Ceremony to Honor Patriotic Georgia Slave Woman"
Atlanta Journal-Constitution
www.ajc.com/news/lifestyles/ceremony-to-honor-patriotic
-georgia-slave-woman/nQMgs

The Official History of Elbert County, 1790–1935 by John H.
McIntosh (Daughters of the American Revolution, 1940)
https://familysearch.org/eng/library/fhlcatalog/supermain
frameset.asp?display=titledetails&titleno=163748&disp=The
+official+history+of+Elbert+County%2C or Google Books

"Stephen Heard (1740–1815)"
New Georgia Encyclopedia
www.georgiaencyclopedia.org/nge/Article.jsp?id=h-2869

Nancy Hart

$\blacklozenge\!\blacklozenge\!\blacklozenge$

THE WAR WOMAN

Nancy Hart could get things done! When Colonel Elijah Clarke, one of the leaders of the Georgia militia, needed information about what the British troops on the other side of the Savannah River were planning, Nancy Hart volunteered to cross the river and find out what she could. The only problem was there was no bridge. That didn't stop "Aunt Nancy," as she was often called.

Described as "six feet high, very muscular, and erect in her gait; her hair light brown," Nancy gathered some logs strewn along the riverside and used those muscles of hers to tie them together with vines to form a raft, which she navigated across the river. She got the information, returned, and told it to the Georgia troops.

That's one of the "Nancy Hart stories," as they're called.

While stories about Nancy are considered legends, the details of her life are not. Nancy Morgan Hart was born Ann Morgan probably in 1735 and nicknamed Nancy by her parents, Thomas and Rebecca Alexander Morgan—Nancy was a popular nickname for those named Ann or Anne.

Since the Hart family lived in Bucks County, Pennsylvania, and later moved to North Carolina, Nancy may have been born in either place. She was related to some prominent people. Her cousin was the frontiersman Daniel Boone, the son of her father's sister, Sarah Morgan, and her husband, Squire Boone. Thomas Hart Benton, who was a US senator from Missouri from 1821 to 1851, was also a relative.

Nancy married Benjamin Hart, who during the Revolution was first a quartermaster and in 1776 became a lieutenant. He served until November 1782. During their life together, Nancy and Benjamin moved from a home in Edgefield, South Carolina, to Elbert, Georgia, and later to Wilkes County, and raised eight children: Morgan, John, Benjamin, Thomas, Samuel, Mark, Sukey, and Keziah.

Nancy was by all accounts a larger-than-life personality. Another Nancy Hart story was published in 1854, 70 years after the end of the Revolution, in Reverend George White's book, *Historical Collections of Georgia*. White claimed he heard the story (and the raft story) from a woman named Mrs. Wyche, whom he described as "a lady far advanced in years who was on terms of intimacy with Mrs. Hart."

As the story goes, when the British were in control of Augusta, Georgia, and Colonel Clarke again wanted to know British plans, Nancy dressed as a man and marched with confidence into a British camp. She pretended to be crazy so as to avoid close inspection, and under this guise was able to gather information about British plans, which she passed on to Colonel Clarke.

Reverend Snead, another man who knew Nancy, shared another Nancy story with Reverend George White, mentioning that Nancy "never failed to be much excited" when she talked of her adventures with the Tories, and had related the following to him firsthand: One day Nancy was at home, busily stirring a pot of boiling soap that was hanging over an open fire, when one of her children "discovered someone from the outside peeping through the crevices of the chimney, and gave a silent intimation of it to Nancy." Nancy suspected it was a Tory.

While she continued stirring, Nancy did talk excitedly and disparagingly about the Tories—supporters of the British—while she kept an eye on the crevice to see if the Tory would look in again. He did. Then, "with the quickness of lightning, she dashed the ladle of boiling soap through the crevice full in the face of the eavesdropper, who taken by surprise, and blinded by the hot soap, screamed and roared at a tremendous rate." Nancy walked outside and made fun of him as she tied him up, and "bound him fast as her prisoner."

The many Nancy Hart stories are hard to believe. That's one reason they're considered legends—stories passed on from one person to another that may be partly true but are probably exaggerated.

Exaggerated yet irresistible! Since Mrs. Wyche knew Nancy Hart, the stories she shared surely have a kernel of truth. How much truth? According to Reverend White's account, another woman, Mrs. T. M. Green, regent of the Kettle Creek chapter of the Daughters of the American Revolution, "said that her father who was born in 1798, lived in the Nancy Hart neighborhood and that she had often heard him tell stories about Nancy Hart; but Mrs. Green admitted that some of the stories 'have of later years been somewhat exaggerated.'"

The most well known of the Nancy Hart stories highlights Nancy's brash, quick-thinking ways. It was told to Elizabeth Ellet, author of the three-volume book *Women of the American Revolution* (1848–1850), who visited Georgia in the 1840s to collect stories about women who participated during the

Revolution—personal stories, heroic stories, stories of every sort. An unnamed but reportedly reputable gentleman shared the story with her.

According to Ellet's version, Tories from the British camp at Augusta came to the area where Nancy lived and "savagely massacred a friend of Nancy's while he was in bed in his own house." The friend was Colonel John Dooly, one of the leaders of the local pro-Revolution militia. The Tories then arrived at Nancy's house. According to Ellet, Nancy was "well known to the Tories, who stood somewhat in fear of her vengeance for any grievance or aggressive act."

After Nancy greeted them, the Tories confronted her with a question: "Did you help a rebel escape from some of our other Tory friends?" Nancy admitted it, and boasted of how she did it. She told them that some days before, she had been alarmed when she had heard sounds of a horse galloping toward her house. She had grabbed her gun, but when she saw that the horseman was a fellow Whig, she had put it down. After the horseman told her that Tories were chasing him, she promptly motioned him to pass through her house and "take to the swamp, and secure himself as well as he could."

After he left, Nancy covered her head so that she appeared to be an old woman, as her children stood watching. When the pursuing Tories knocked on her door, she opened it and asked "why they disturbed a sick, lone woman." When the men told about their search for a man on a horse, she said she had seen "someone on a sorrel horse turn out of the path into the woods." She was, of course, lying to them, and the men headed off in the opposite direction of the way the fugitive had gone.

The Tories listened to Nancy as she related her tale, laughing as she did. After the other Tories had left, she told them, she had pulled the rag off her head and said to her children, "If they hadn't er been so lofty minded—but had looked on the ground . . . they would have seen his horse tracks up to that door, as plain as you can see the tracks on this here floor, and out of t'other door down the path to the swamp."

According to Ellet's telling, after the men heard Nancy boast about how she had tricked their fellow Tories, they demanded she cook a meal for them. Nancy complained that the other Tories had stolen all her chickens and pigs and that she hardly had enough to feed her own family. On hearing that, one of the Tories spied an old turkey walking in her yard, shot it, and told her to cook it for them. "She stormed and swore awhile" and then started to clean it.

As she was preparing the meal, her 12-year-old daughter, Sukey, helped her, as did one of the Tories. Nancy joked with the helping Tory, and the men began drinking the liquor they'd brought with them. At the same time, though, Nancy was devising a plan. Under the guise of needing water for cooking, she asked Sukey to go outside to fetch some at the spring. Yet it wasn't the water that Nancy really wanted. She wanted Sukey to pick up the conch shell kept on a tree stump by the spring and blow in it. Settlers in that area used the shells like musical instruments and to relay information. For example, one sound meant to be on the alert; another sound meant to come at once. Sukey used the conch to alert her father and neighbors to the Tories' presence.

Meanwhile, inside the house, as the men started to enjoy themselves and relax, they "stacked their arms where they were in view and within reach." Nancy stealthily took one of the muskets and slid it out through a space between the logs of the cabin. Then she slid another. She again sent Sukey out to the spring for "water." This time Sukey used the conch shell to tell her father and neighbors to come at once.

Inside, as Nancy tried to take the third musket, "the whole party sprang to their feet." Nancy responded quickly, raising the musket and pointing it at the Tories. She warned them that she "would kill the first man who approached her." When one of them moved toward her, she shot him dead. Nancy then grabbed one of the other muskets, warning the Tories again as she pointed it at them.

When Sukey returned with the pail of water, she announced, "Daddy and them will soon be here." The Tories must have realized the danger and reality of the situation—that it would be easier to fight against one woman than a group of men. One of them moved. Nancy shot again, and killed him. Sukey handed Nancy one of the other muskets and Nancy demanded that the Tories surrender their "d_____ tory carcasses to a whig woman."

Benjamin Hart and his neighbors arrived and wanted to shoot the remaining Tories, but Nancy insisted "shooting was

Nancy Hart and the Tories.
Pioneer Mothers of America, *1912*

too good for them." Nancy, Benjamin, and the others took the remaining Tories outside and hung them.

Ellet's story inspired artists to depict the scene, which boosted its legend.

This is surely a dramatic and memorable story. But is it true? In 1825, some 23 years earlier, and 40 years after the Revolution, the story about Nancy and the Tories first appeared in print, in the *Milledgeville Southern Reporter*, and was later copied in two other publications.

It was a much simpler version of the tale. As it went, one day Nancy was at home with her children when six Tories—locals who were pro-British—stopped by her house. They demanded that she cook them a meal. Before long, "smoking venison, hoe-cakes, and fresh honeycomb" were on the table. The men had just stacked their guns and sat down to eat when Nancy seized one of their guns. She pointed it at them, "cocked it, and with a blazing oath declared she would blow out the brains of the first mortal that offered to rise or taste a mouthful!" While the men sat captive, she sent her son to fetch some local Whigs, support-ers of the Revolution. According to the *Southern Reporter*, the Tories, either "uncertain because of her cross-eyes which one she was aiming at, or transfixed by her ferocity, remained quiet." The Whigs soon arrived and dealt with the Tories "according to the rules of the times."

On one point, Reverend Snead, who knew Nancy, com-mented that "she was positively not cross-eyed."

A third version of this same story was told by George R. Gilmer in an 1851 speech. He told of three Tories who snuck up to Nancy's cabin in the summer of 1780. They wanted break-fast. "When the Tories sat down to eat they stacked their guns, whereupon Nancy grabbed one of the weapons, cocked it, and marched the Tories off to Clark's station."

Which story of Nancy and the Tories is most accurate, the one printed in the *Milledgeville Southern Reporter* in 1825, Elizabeth Ellet's 1848 version, or Gilmer's from 1851? It is hard to tell. One argument against the more dramatic versions is that quite a few historians visited the area where Nancy lived in the 50 years after the Revolution seeking evidence of actions of individual people in the war. Yet a two-volume history of Georgia didn't mention her, and other histories only included brief comments or noted that "the stories related in fancy sketches ought to be taken with some grains of allowance." The Nancy stories would likely have faded away had they not been retold in 1901 by storyteller Joel Chandler Harris, author of the Uncle Remus stories, and by the publicity efforts of the National Society Daughters of the American Revolution.

In 1912, however, a discovery gave rise to much speculation about the visiting Tories story. During the construction of the Elberton and Eastern Railroad, workmen digging near the location of Nancy Hart's cabin discovered six human skeletons. Were they the remains of the Tories slain by Nancy and her husband and his neighbors? Was this proof? Historians are not sure. As expressed by E. Merton Coulter, a prominent Georgia historian who explored the truth of the Nancy stories in the 1950s, "Yes, there was a Nancy Hart and there will always be a Nancy Hart tradition."

That tradition is evident in the naming of Hart County, Georgia, after her, the only county in Georgia named for a woman, as well as Lake Hartwell, the Nancy Hart Highway, various schools, hotels, and more.

After the end of the Revolutionary War, and after the death of Nancy's husband, according to Reverend White, Nancy "consoled herself, like most other good wives who have the luck, by marrying a young man," and moved out West with him.

Another Nancy Hart story? In fact, Nancy never remarried but lived with her son John and his wife after Benjamin's death and moved to Kentucky with them. After John's death, she continued living with his widow.

When did Nancy die? It's hard to know. No contemporary record of her death has been found. It might have been in 1815 or 1820. Nancy would have been 80 or 85 then, and during both those years, a memorable natural event occurred. According to one historian, "A descendent of Nancy's wrote in 1901 that at the time of her funeral there was a total eclipse of the sun."

A total eclipse of the sun? The start of another story? Probably not, but a fitting send-off for Nancy.

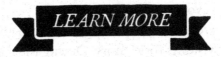

LEARN MORE

"The Nancy Hart Story"
Georgia Stories
Georgia Public Broadcasting
www.gpb.org/georgiastories/story/nancy_hart_story

"The Nancy Hart Story—Historical Documents"
Georgia Stories
Georgia Public Broadcasting
www.gpb.org/georgiastories/docs/the_nancy_hart_story-13

"Nancy Morgan Hart (1735-1830)"
National Women's History Museum
www.nwhm.org/education-resources/biography/biographies
/nancy-morgan-hart/

Women of the American Revolution, Vol. II, by Elizabeth F. Ellet, contains a chapter on Nancy Hart.
http://archive.org or Google Books

Acknowledgments

Delving into the stories and lives of those who lived more than 200 years ago presents tremendous challenges. "Thank you" doesn't express the depth of my appreciation for the efforts of those who provided information and insights, suggested changes, and reviewed chapters.

I owe much to so many for their comments and contributions including Daniel E. Krieger, Professor of History, Cal Poly State University, and Liz Krieger; Michael Scoggins, historian, Culture & Heritage Museums, Historic Brattonsville; Vincent Dacquino; Marnie Pehrson; Marsha Mullin, Chief Curator, The Hermitage; Greg Nathan and Jessica Ebeling-Gulley of the Edenton Historical Commission; Dennis O'Neill, President, Cupola House Association; Diane Cronin and members of the Pepperell Historical Commission; Ansley Herring Wegner, Research Historian, North Carolina Office of Archives and History; Nancy A. Pope, Curator/Historian, National Postal Museum; Harlan Green, Head of Special Collections, Addlestone Library, College of Charleston; Nic Butler, Historian, Charleston County Public Library; Douglas Wayne Harvey, West Virginia SAR;

Shirley Schofield, Sharon Historical Society, Inc.; Steve Connolly; Erica Lindamood and Emily Curran, Old South Meeting House; Vivian Bruce Conger, Department of History, Ithaca College; Alexander Rose; Ray Raphael; Vincent Carretta, University of Maryland; Sarah Cunningham, Ninety Six National Historic Site; Patricia Bonomi, Historian Emerita, New York University; Susan Branson, Syracuse University; Wayne K. Bodle, Department of History, Indiana University of Pennsylvania; Edwin Burrows, Distinguished Professor of History at Brooklyn College, and Dr. Owen S. Ireland, Distinguished Teaching Professor, SUNY Brockport. Thanks as well to Eric Blevins, Photographer, North Carolina Museum of History; John Minichiello, imaging specialist at John Carter Brown Library; and Sidney Thompson of the Greenville County Historical Society. Heartfelt thanks to my history professor at Santa Clara University, George Giacomini, who spurred my interest in history, and to my classmate, Thomas Bender, NYU, who was instrumental in connecting me with historians who provided comments and insights. A special thank you to Steven Brown, Hargrett Rare Book & Manuscript Library, Lee Ann Caldwell, director of the Center for the Study of Georgia History at Georgia Regents University, and Peggy Galis for their joint efforts in uncovering details about Mammy Kate.

Thanks to the team at Chicago Review Press. My editor, Lisa Reardon, a wonderfully measured person, inspired me to bring life to the stories of the women of the revolution. I also thank publisher Cynthia Sherry for her continuing support, Sarah Olson for her stunning design, Amelia Estrich, and the rest of the team. Thanks as well to my agency Sheree Bykofsky Associates and to my agent, Janet Rosen, who always goes out of her way for me.

Thanks to Alan Kaplan and his students of Hamilton High School, Los Angeles, for their review of chapters and astute comments, and to the many other students who provided comments, especially Francesca Reale, for her review of the first chapter.

I am indebted to my friends Michelle Markel, Cyndy Turnage and Peter Kors, Mary Rose O'Leary and Rachel Clark, Judy Hammond and Bill Megalos, Jose Ramos, Hugo Garcia and Sue Mattor for their constant support. I am especially appreciative of the help with images from Val Riordan, Carolyn Brown, and Scott Schneider; to Scotty Embree and Joanna Exacoustos, who pitched in by reading drafts of chapters; Jane Stubbs, who helped in so many ways; and Charles Dixson for his encouragement. Thanks to the folks at Joni's Coffee Roasting Cafe, where much of the book was written, especially Richard Block and to members of the book club. Hats off to Carlos Casey for his research help, and to Lana Cohen and Alice Kors for their careful attention to detail and help with notes and the bibliography.

As always, thanks to my brothers and sisters: Pat, Mike, Kevin, Jim, Katie, and to all the other Caseys, Weltes, and Andersons, and to my irrepressible nieces and nephews.

Glossary

artillery: Large guns, cannons, used to shoot over a long distance.

bayonet: A knife or sword that could be attached to a musket.

broadside: A poster or large piece of paper printed only on one side, used during the colonial period to advertise or to announce events or proclamations. The Declaration of Independence was printed as a broadside on July 4, 1776.

camp follower: Civilians (those who were not in an army) who traveled with the troops and provided services such as cooking, laundering, or nursing.

Continental Army: The American army that was authorized by the Continental Congress during the American Revolution.

Continental Congress: The governing body of the colonies during the Revolutionary War, made up of delegate representatives from the individual colonies. The First Continental Congress met in 1774. The Second Continental Congress met from 1775 to 1789 and issued the Declaration of Independence.

dragoon: A soldier who could fight on horseback or on foot.

freedman: A freed slave.

guerilla fighting/warfare: A nontraditional way of fighting that involves ambushes and raids.

Hessians: German soldiers hired and paid by the British to fight for them and alongside their soldiers during the American Revolution.

Some of the 30,000 Hessians hired by the British fought in almost every campaign.

loyalist: A person born in America who was loyal to the British and wanted America to remain loyal to the British king.

mercenaries: Soldiers who are paid to fight.

militia: During the American Revolution, healthy men were required to be part of local militias, fighting forces, to defend their homes and towns. These citizen soldiers weren't part of the formal Continental Army.

minuteman: The name given to militiamen in the year prior to the outbreak of the American Revolution. They were expected to be ready at a minute's notice to defend their homes, towns, and cities.

musket: A weapon used by foot soldiers during the American Revolution that fired one or more round, ammunition balls at a time. Some had attached bayonets, a knife or sword, used for close fighting.

muster: To mobilize troops in preparation for battle.

parole: A pledge given by prisoners of war not to bear arms against the other side or encourage others to do so in exchange for being released.

patriot: Colonists who rebelled against the British during the American Revolution. Also called rebels or Whigs.

privateer: A shipowner licensed by the government to capture enemy ships and their cargo.

Quaker: A member of the Religious Society of Friends, a religious group that opposes war.

Royal Army: British Army.

sabotage: An intentional action aimed at damaging, disrupting, or destroying something to gain a political or military advantage. To vandalize.

tarred and feathered: A punitive act of covering a person with tar and feathers as a way of demonstrating disapproval of his or her actions. The tar and feathers were hard to remove.

Tory: An American who supported the British side during the American Revolution. Also called a loyalist.

treason: The crime of betraying one's country.

Whig: An American who supported the American Revolution.

winter quarters: Places where armies camped during the winter.

Notes

————————————————

PART ONE: RESISTERS, SUPPORTERS, AND RESCUERS

Penelope Barker: Steeping the Brew

"charming in its refinement and culture": Dillard, *The North Carolina Booklet*, 2.

"one of the most fashionable modes of entertaining": Ibid., 8.

"the ladies would gossip and spin, and reel": Ibid., 10.

"discuss the political issues of the day": Ibid., 10.

"one of those lofty, intrepid, high-born women": Ibid., 12.

"a brilliant conversationalist": Ibid.

"Edenton, North Carolina, Oct. 25, 1774. As we cannot": Halsey, *The Boston Port Bill As Pictured By a Contemporary London Cartoonist*, 314.

"a society leader of her day": *The North Carolina Booklet*, 12.

The Provincial Deputies: *Morning Chronicle and London Advertiser,* January 15, 1775.

London Queen Square: Dillard, *The North Carolina Booklet*, 8.

"Is there a female congress": Ibid., 204.

The 51 signers: Haines, *The Boston Port Bill As Pictured By a Contemporary London Cartoonist*, 314–315.

Phillis Wheatley: The Slave Who Proclaimed a Revolution

"several robust, healthy females": Odell, *Memoir and Poems of Phillis Wheatley, a Native African and a Slave*, 9.

"humble and modest demeanor": Ibid.

"'TWAS mercy brought me from my Pagan land": Wheatley, *Phillis Wheatley Complete Writings*, 60.

"Rule thou in peace, our father": Carretta, *Phillis Wheatley*, 69.

"With unexpected infamy disgraced": Ibid., 77.

"Boston, May 10, 1773 Saturday": Ibid., 135.

I mourn for Health deny'd: Ibid., 62.

"Let us imagine the loss of a parent": Ibid., 153.

Proceed, great chief, with virtue: Carretta, *Phillis Wheatley*, 155–156.

"I recollect nothing else worth": *The Papers of George Washington, Revolutionary War Series*, vol. 3, *1 January 1776–31 March 1776*, ed. Philander D. Chase. Charlottesville: University Press of Virginia, 1988, pp. 286–291.

"Cambridge, Mass. February 28, 1776": George Washington Papers at the Library of Congress, 1741–1799: Series 3h, Varick Transcripts.

"Let virtue reign": Wheatley, *Phillis Wheatley Complete Writings*, 30.

"no birth, baptismal, or": Carretta, *Phillis Wheatley*, 177.

Mary Katherine Goddard: A Patriotic Publisher

"Baltimore: April 26. We have": Hudak, *Early American Women Printers and Publishers*, 341.

"Able-bodied freemen from the ages of 17": Ibid., 350.

"Mrs. Smith, in the 109th year": Ibid., 333.

"SIXTY DOLLARS Reward . . . Ran away": July 6, 1779, *Maryland Journal*, Library of Congress.

"George Washington of Mt. Vernon": Wroth, *A History of Printing in Colonial Maryland 1686-1771*, 129.

"Thirty Dollars Reward": July 6, 1779, *Maryland Journal*, Library of Congress.

"Wants A Place": July 6, 1779, *Maryland Journal*, Library of Congress.

"This was by no means the first": Hudak, *Early American Women Printers and Publishers*, 348.

Elizabeth Hutchinson Jackson: Mother to the End

"snapping blue eyes": James, *The Life of Andrew Jackson*, 4.
"In Congress, July 4, 1776": Ibid., 16.
"I was well fitted, being a good rider": Ibid., 20.
"Make friends by being honest": Booraem, *Young Hickory*, 108.
"I felt utterly alone": James, *The Life of Andrew Jackson*, 29.
"The memory of my mother": Brands, *Andrew Jackson*, 32.

Esther Reed and Sarah Franklin Bache: Supporters of the Troops

"My dear Mr. Reed was": Reed, *Life and Correspondence of Joseph Reed*, 259.
"If I live happy in the midst of my family": Reed, *Sentiments of An American Woman*.
"render the condition": Reed, *Life and Correspondence of Joseph Reed*, 265.
"They normally would not": E-mail from Vivian Bruce Conger.
"People were obliged to": Evans, *Weathering the Storm*, 289.
"The gentlemen were also honored": Ibid., 288–289.
"All ranks of society seem to have joined": Green, *The Pioneer Mothers of America*, 150.
"The ladies are anxious for": Reed, *Life and Correspondence of Joseph Reed*, 262.
"If I am in having the concurrence": Marsh, "The Purist Patriotism."
"an idea prevails among the ladies": Reed, *Life and Correspondence of Joseph Reed*, 264.
"a taste of hard money may be productive": Ibid., 265.
"had not the most distant wish": Ibid., 266.
"I shall now endeavor": Ibid., 267.
"Our dear little children are pretty well": Ibid., 268.
"In memory of Esther": Ibid., 269.
"I have been busily employed in cutting out shirts": Ibid., 270.
"We packed up the shirts in three boxes": Ibid., 270.
"The army ought not to regret their sacrifices": Sparks, *The Writings of George Washington*, 408.
"TO MRS. FRANCIS, MRS. HILLEGAS, MRS. CLARKSON": Ibid., 408.

Elizabeth Burgin: The Rescuer Who Became a Fugitive

"Friday, 13th of December, 1776": Commager, *The Spirit of Seventy-Six*, 856.

"On July 17th I was": Burgin, *Letter to Reverend James Colville*, National Archives.

"carried out Major van": Ibid.

"Letter to Major Benjamin Tallmadge": "Spy Letters of the American Revolution" in the Clinton Collection from the Clements Library

"George Higby was taken": Burgin, *Letter to Reverend James Calville*, National Archives.

"Through the behalf of friends, I got on Long Island": Ibid.

"I am now Sir, very desolate, without money": Ibid.

"Head Quarters Morristown": *George Washington Papers* at the Library of Congress, 1741–1799: Series 3a, Varick Transcripts.

"praying to be employed": *Journals of the Continental Congress, 1774–1789*, Volume 20, 718.

"I received a kind letter from your aid": *George Washington Papers* at the Library of Congress, 1741–1799: Series 4. General Correspondence, 1697–1799.

PART TWO: SPIES

Lydia Darragh: The Listener Who Alerted the General

"A number of troops have gone out of town": Menkevich, "Agent Lydia Darragh-Intelligence Operative," 4.

"There is talk to day": Ibid., 3.

"The Subscriber, living in Second street": Ibid., 12.

"to have all her family in bed": Darrach, "Lydia Darragh, One of the Heroines of the Revolution," *City History Society of Philadelphia*, 389.

"into a closet, separated": Ibid., 389.

"Washington's army, and with their": Ibid., 390.

"did not tell her husband": Ibid., 391.

"was greatly surprised to see": Ibid., 391.

"In Autumn of 1777 the American": Boudinot, *The Life, Public Services, Addresses and Letters of Elias Boudinot*, 68.

"On comparing this with other information": Ibid., 68–69.

"called her to the council room": Ibid., 391.

"She replied: 'No, they were all asleep'": Ibid., 391–393.
"'I never told a lie about it'": Ibid., 393.
"In the course of last week": Ibid., 400.
"The story has been discredited": Ibid., 393.

Anna Smith Strong: Petticoats and Handkerchiefs

"[I] think by the assistance of": Rose, *Washington's Spies*, 247.
"In the case of 355" Kilmeade, *George Washington's Secret Six*, 93.
"Folklore is an": E-mail from Beverly C. Tyler.
"Private dispatches are frequently": Rose, *Washington's Spies*, 247.
"the problem [for the British]": Ibid., 247.
"correctly perceived that": Ibid., 234.

Dicey Langston: A Whig in a Land of Tories

"She declared that her own body": Ellet, *Women of the American Revolution*, 288.
"Shoot me if you dare. I will not tell you": Ibid., 289.
"threw up his hand, and": Ibid., 289.
"Do you think so?": Ibid., 291.
"pronounced her worthy of being the sister of James Langston": Ibid., 291.
"Mrs. Laodicea Springfield, aged 71 years": *Greenville (SC) Mountaineer*, June 10, 1837.

PART THREE: SABOTEURS

Prudence Wright: Leader of the Pitchfork Brigade

"without stopping to unyoke his oxen": Fischer, *Paul Revere's Ride*, 157.
"meet a force of English and lead them": Shattuck, *Prudence Wright and the Women Who Guarded the Bridge*, 35.
"Soon there appeared one on horseback": Butler, *History of the Town of Groton*, 336–337.
"immediately arrested, unhorsed, searched": Ibid., 336.
"resolutely determined, that no foe to freedom": Ibid., 336.
"a force of English": Shattuck, *Prudence Wright and the Women Who Guarded the Bridge*, 35.
"seized the reins of their horses": Ibid., 33.

"I recognize Prude's voice and she would": Ibid., 36.
"The men were dismounted and searched": Ibid., 36.
"to Groton to the Committee of Safety": Ibid., 35–36.
"Not one further step I ride!": Ibid., 33.
"her brother Thomas [who] was never seen": Ibid., 34–35.
"The women surrounded him": Ibid., 34.
"marched their prisoner": Citation TK
"fellow townsmen to be loyalists for Tories": Ibid., 34.

Sybil Ludington: On Star Under the Stars

"fat from the burning": Bailey, *History of Danbury, Conn 1684-1896*, 69.
"In this emergency": Johnson, *Colonel Henry Ludington*, 89.
"The British are burning": SOURCE TK
"the greater part of the force were": Bailey, *History of Danbury, Conn 1684–1896*, 69.
"spend the Sabbath leisurely in Danbury": Ibid., 72.
"that the rebels under Wooster and Arnold": Ibid., 72.
"Flames seemed to burst out simultaneously": Ibid., 73.
"The enemy's loss is judged to be more": Ibid., 80.
"There is no extravagance in comparing": Johnson, *Colonel Henry Ludington*, 90.

Mary Lindley Murray: Wine, Cake, and a Getaway

"a grand public breakfast": Murray, *In the Olden Time*, 5.
"nearly thirty people": Ibid., 5.
"silk jacket": Ibid., 5.
"mirth and pleasure echoed": Ibid., 5.
"My mother was a woman": Ellet, *Women of the American Revolution*, 375.
"all of a sudden there came": Martin, *Private Yankee Doodle*, 34.
"he plunged his horse among them": McCullough, *1776*, 212.
"I saw a Hessian sever a rebel's head": McCullough, *1776*, 30.
"It so happened that a body": Thacher, *Military Journal During the American Revolutionary War, from 1775–1783*, 70.
"magnificent avenue of elms": Murray, *In the Olden Time*, 5.
"Mrs. Murray treated them with cake and wine": Thacher, *Military Journal During the American Revolutionary War*, 60.

"[was] joking her about": Ibid., 60.

"might have turned the laugh on him": Ellet, *Women of the American Revolution*, 340.

"Most fortunately, the British": Thacher, *Military Journal During the American Revolutionary War*, 60.

Grace and Rachel Martin: Masquerading Hostesses

"Go boys, fight for your country!": Ellet, *Women of the American Revolution*, 277.

"'Grace,' said Mrs. Rachel": Green, *The Pioneer Mothers of America*, 339.

"With rifles over their shoulders": Ibid., 339.

"As they came close to the spot": Ellet, *Women of the American Revolution*, 275.

"returning so soon after": Ibid., 276.

"departed the next morning": Ibid., 276.

PART FOUR: SOLDIERS AND
DEFENDERS OF THE HOME FRONT

Elizabeth "Betty" Zane: Fleet-Footed Girl to the Rescue

"a fair-haired, finely formed girl": Green, *Pioneer Mothers of America*, 447.

"about the exploit of Betsy Zane": Hintzen, "Betty Zane, Lydia Boggs, and Molly Scott," www.wvculture.org.

Deborah Sampson Gannett: Undercover Soldier

"Poise—Firelock!": Young, *Masquerade*, 205.

"Deborah was about five feet eight": Furbee, *Women of the American Revolution*, 60.

Mrs. Gannett's (Late Deborah Sampson): Young, *Masquerade*, 203.

"Thus I became an actor in that important drama": Ibid., 221.

"the perils and inconvenience of a girl in her teens": Ibid., 221.

"Mrs. Deborah Gannet of Sharon informs": Massachusetts Historical Society, http://www.masshist.org/database/326.

Rebecca Motte: A Straight-Arrow Heroine

"[To think] of one so": Ellet, *Women of the American Revolution*, 150.

"bow was put into the hands of Nathan": Simms, *The Life of Francis Marion*, 239.

"Now I have told you all the news": Harrison, *A Charleston Album*, 43.

"a high crowned ruffled mobcap": Ibid., 43.

Martha Bratton: "It was I who did it."

"He is in Sumter's army": Ellet, *Women of the American Revolution*, 144.

"I beg of you to consult Mrs. Bratton": Scoggins, *The Day it Rained Militia*, 118.

"Madam, you were sent for": Ibid., 119.

"My Mother, who was skilled in concocting": Ibid.

"laughed at my Mother": Ibid.

"It's important to note": Interview with Michael Scoggins.

"It was I who did it": Ellet, *Women of the American Revolution*, 247.

"Let the consequences be what it will": Ibid., 247.

PART FIVE: LEGENDARY LADIES

Molly Pitcher: "Possible Mollies" Mary Ludwig Hayes and Margaret Cochran Corbin

"One of the camp women": Stryker, *The Battle of Monmouth*, 189.

"A woman whose husband belonged": Martin, *Ordinary Courage*, 80.

"While Captain Molly was": Custis, *Recollections and Private Memoirs of Washington*, 225.

"Thirsty, weary soldiers calling out": Somerville, *Women and the American Revolution*, 6.

"The wife of a gunner in the American Army": Caption from Currier & Ives print, "The Heroine of Monmouth."

"homely in appearance": Somerville, *Women and the American Revolution*, 11.

"Judge of his surprise when": Green, *Pioneer Mothers of America*, 224–225.

"Resolved—That Margaret Corbin": Somerville, *Women and the American Revolution*, 12.

"the famous Irishwoman": Ibid., 13.
"I have procured a place": Ibid., 15.
"was also furnished with old bed-sacks": Ibid., 15.
"was saluted as 'Captain'": Ibid., 15.
"MARGARET CORBIN—THE FIRST": Ibid., 17.
  "she should have the means": Dann, *The Revolution Remembered*, 242–250.
"was not afraid of the cannonballs?": Ibid.

Mammy Kate: Unlikely Rescuer

"The British captured Governor Heard": Hampton, *A Family History*, a handwritten letter, Hargrett Rare Book & Manuscript Library, University of Georgia.
"The idea that Mammy Kate": Interview with Peggy Galis, November 18, 2012.
"Augusta was not": Interview with Lee Ann Caldwell, July 3, 2014.
"Perhaps Mammy Kate": Ibid.
"One of his faithful slaves would": Peel, *Historical Collections of the Joseph Habersham Chapter, Daughters of the American Revolution*, 279.
"One morning, carrying on her head": McIntosh, *The Official History of Elbert County 1790–1935*, 23.
"She [Aunt Kate] managed to get": Peel, *Historical Collections of the Joseph Habersham Chapter*, 280.
"The night previous to this": Ibid., 280.
"While they were traveling homeward": McIntosh, *The Official History of Elbert County*, 23.
"Paternalistic owners often showed kindnesses": Caldwell interview.
"When I was growing up": Galis interview.
"We used to talk about Mammy": Ibid.
"The house my grandmother": Ibid.
"She [Aunt Kate] used to act as a spy for her master": Caldwell interview.
"the result of a cold caught": Hampton, *A Family History*.
"The story we always heard": Galis interview.
"When Aunt Kate died": Hampton, *A Family History*.
"She and anyone in his household": Caldwell interview.

Nancy Hart: The War Woman

"six feet high, very muscular": White, *Historical Collections of Georgia*, 441.

"a lady far advanced in years": Ibid., 446.

"never failed to be much excited": Ibid., 441.

"discovered someone from the outside": Ibid., 441.

"with the quickness of lightning": Ibid., 442.

"bound him fast as her prisoner": Ibid., 442.

"said that her father who": Coulter, "Nancy Hart, Georgia Heroine of the Revolution," *The Georgia Historical Quarterly*, Vol. 39, No. 2, June 1955.

"savagely massacred a friend": Ellet, *Women of the American Revolution*, Vol. II, 264.

"well known to the tories": Ibid., 263–264.

"take to the swamp, and secure himself": Ibid., 265.

"why they disturbed a sick, lone woman": Ibid.

"someone on a sorrel horse": Ibid.

"If they hadn't er been so lofty": Ibid., 266.

"She stormed and swore awhile": Ibid.

"stacked their arms where they": Ibid., 267.

"the whole party sprang to their feet": Ibid., 268.

"would kill the first man who": Ibid.

"Daddy and them will soon be here": Ibid.

"d___ Tory carcasses to a Whig woman": Ibid., 269.

"shooting was too good for them": Ibid.

"smoking venison, hoe-cakes": Coulter, "Nancy Hart, Georgia Heroine of the Revolution," 142.

"cocked it, and with a blazing oath": Ibid.

"uncertain because of her cross-eyes": Ibid.

"according to the rules of the times": Ibid.

"she was positively not cross-eyed": White, *Historical Collections of Georgia*, 441.

"When the Tories": Coulter, "Nancy Hart, Georgia Heroine of the Revolution," 144.

"the stories related": Scott, "Nancy Hart: 'Too Good Not to Tell Again,'" in *Georgia Women: Their Lives and Times*, 42.

"consoled herself, like most other good": White, *Historical Collections of Georgia*, 442.

"A descendent of Nancy's wrote in 1901": Coulter, "Nancy Hart," 125.

Bibliography

BOOKS

Allen, Thomas B. *George Washington, Spymaster: How the Americans Outspied the British and Won the American Revolution.* Washington, DC: National Geographic Children's Books, 2004.

Allison, Robert J. *The American Revolution.* New York: Oxford University Press, 2011.

Bailey, James Montgomery. "History of Danbury, Conn. 1684–1896." Chapter in *Notes and Manuscript Left by James Montgomery Bailey.* Compiled with additions by Susan Benedict Hill. New York: Burr Printing House, 1896.

Berkin, Carol. *Revolutionary Mothers: Women in the Struggle for America's Independence.* New York: Alfred A. Knopf, 2005.

Blumenthal, Walter Hart. *Women Camp Followers of the Revolution.* New York: Arno Press, 1974.

Bodle, Wayne. *The Valley Forge Winter: Civilians and Soldiers in War.* University Park, Pennsylvania: Pennsylvania State University Press, 2002.

Bohrer, Melissa Lukeman. *Glory, Passion, and Principle: The Story of Eight Remarkable Women at the Core of the American Revolution.* New York: Atria Books, 2003.

Booraem, Hendrik. *Young Hickory: The Making of Andrew Jackson.* Dallas: Taylor Trade Publishing, 2001.

Boudinot, J. J., ed. *The Life of Public Services, Addresses and Letters of Elias Boudinot, LL.D., President of the Continental Congress, Vol. 1.* New York: Houghton, Mifflin and Company, 1896.

Bracken, Jeanne Munn. *Women in the American Revolution.* Boston: History Compass, 2009.

Brands, H. W. *Andrew Jackson: His Life and Times.* New York: Doubleday, 2005.

Burrows, Edwin G. *Forgotten Patriots: The Untold Story of American Prisoners during the Revolutionary War.* New York: Basic Books, 2008.

Butler, Caleb. *History of the Town of Groton, Including Pepperell and Shirley.* Boston: Press of T. R. Marvin, 1848.

Carretta, Vincent. *Phillis Wheatley: Biography of a Genius in Bondage.* Athens, GA: University of Georgia Press, 2011.

Chapman, John A. *History of Edgefield County From the Earliest Settlements to 1897.* Newberry, South Carolina: Elbert H. Aull, Publisher and Printer, 1897.

Chirhart, Ann Short and Betty Wood, eds. *Georgia Women: Their Lives and Times.* Vol. 1. Athens, Georgia: University of Georgia Press, 2009.

Clement, J. *Noble Deeds of American Women; With Biographical Sketches of Some of the More Prominent.* New York: Geo. H. Derby & Co, 1851.

Coleman, Kenneth. *The American Revolution in Georgia, 1763–1789.* Athens, GA: University of Georgia Press, 1958.

Collins, Gail. *America's Women: 400 Years of Dolls, Drudges, Helpmates, and Heroines.* New York: William Morrow, 2003.

Commager, Henry Steele and Richard B. Morris, eds. *The Spirit of Seventy-Six: The Story of the American Revolution as Told by Participants, Vol. 1.* New York: Bobbs-Merrill Company Inc., 1968.

Cotton, Sally S. *History of the North Carolina Federation of Women's Clubs, 1901–1925.* Raleigh, NC: Edwards & Broughton, 1925.

Custis, George Washington Parke. *Recollections and Private Memoirs of Washington.* New York: Derby & Jackson, 1860.

Dacquino, Vincent T. *Hauntings of the Hudson River Valley: An Investigative Journey.* Charleston, SC: The History Press, 2007.

———. *Sybil Ludington: Discovering the Life of a Revolutionary War Hero.* Fleischmanns, NY: Purple Mountain Press, 2008.

————. *Sybil Ludington: The Call to Arms*. Fleischmanns, NY: Purple Mountain Press, 2000.

Dann, John C, ed. *The Revolution Remembered: Eyewitness Accounts of the War for Independence*. Chicago: The University of Chicago Press, 1980.

Darrach, Henry. *Lydia Darragh: One of the Heroines of the Revolution*. Philadelphia: City History Society of Philadelphia, 1916.

Davis, Burke. *Old Hickory: A Life of Andrew Jackson*. New York: Dial Press, 1977.

Depauw, Linda Grant. *Founding Mothers: Women of America in the Revolutionary Era*. Boston: Houghton Mifflin, 1975.

Diamant, Lincoln, ed. *Revolutionary Women: In the War for American Independence*. Westport, CT: Praeger, 1998.

Dorwart, Jeffery M. *Cape May County, New Jersey: The Making of an American Resort Community*. New Brunswick, NJ: Rutgers University Press, 1992.

Drachman, Virginia G. *Enterprising Women: 250 Years of American Business*. Chapel Hill, NC: University of North Carolina Press, 2002.

Egle, William Henry. *Some Pennsylvania Women During the War of the Revolution*. Harrisburg, PA: Harrisburg Publishing Company, 1898.

Ellet, Elizabeth F.. *Woman of the American Revolution*. Vols. 1–3. New York: Baker and Scribner, 1848–1850.

Ellis, Joseph J. *His Excellency: George Washington*. New York: Alfred A Knopf, 2004.

Evans, Elizabeth. *Weathering the Storm: Women of the American Revolution*. New York: Charles Scribner's Sons, 1975.

Fischer, David Hackett. *Paul Revere's Ride*. New York: Oxford University Press, 1994.

Fleming, Thomas J. *Everybody's Revolution: A New Look at the People Who Won America's Freedom*. New York: Scholastic Nonfiction, 2006.

Flick, Alexander C. *Loyalism in New York During the American Revolution*. New York: Columbia University Press, 1901.

Frank, Lisa Tendrich, ed. *An Encyclopedia of American Women at War: From the Home Front to the Battlefields*. Vols. 1–3. Santa Barbara, CA: ABC-CLIO, 2013.

Furbee, Mary R. *Women of the American Revolution*. San Diego: Lucent Books, 1999.

Garrison, Webb. *Great Stories of the American Revolution: Unusual, Interesting Stories of the Exhilarating Era When a Nation Was Born.* Nashville: Rutledge Hill Press, 1993.

Green, Harry Clinton, and Mary Wolcott Green. *The Pioneer Mothers of America.* Vols. 1–3. New York: G. P. Putnam's Sons, 1912.

Halsey, R. T. Haines, Philip Dawes, and John Henry Nash. *The Boston Port Bill as Pictured by a Contemporary London Cartoonist.* New York: The Grolier Club, Gilliss Press, 1904.

Harrison, Margaret Hayne. *A Charleston Album.* Rindge, NH: Richard R. Smith Publisher Inc., 1953.

Hays, Louise Frederick. *Hero of Hornet's Nest: A Biography of Elijah Clark, 1733–1799.* New York: Stratford House, 1946.

Hominick, Judy, and Jeanne Spreier. *Ride for Freedom: The Story of Sybil Ludington.* New York: Silver Moon Press, 2001.

Hudak, Leona M. *Early American Women Printers and Publishers, 1639–1820.* Metuchen, NJ: The Scarecrow Press Inc., 1978.

Ingle, Sheila. *Fearless Martha: A Daughter of the American Revolution.* Spartanburg, SC: Hub City Press, 2011.

James, Edward T. *Notable American Women, 1607–1950: A Biographical Dictionary.* Vol. 1. Cambridge: Belknap Press of Harvard University Press, 1971.

James, Marquis. *The Life of Andrew Jackson.* New York: The Bobbs-Merrill Company, 1938.

Johnson, Joseph. *Traditions and Reminiscences, Chiefly of the American Revolution in the South: Including Biographical Sketches, Incidents and Anecdotes.* Charleston, SC: Walker & James, 1851.

Johnson, Willis Fletcher. *Colonel Henry Ludington: A Memoir.* New York: Printed by his grandchildren Lavinia Elizabeth Ludington and Charles Henry Ludington, 1907.

Kallen, Stuart A. *Life During the American Revolution.* San Diego: Lucent Books, 2002.

Kalman, Bobbie. *18th Century Clothing.* New York: Crabtree Publishing Co., 1993.

Kerber, Linda K. *Women of the Republic: Intellect and Ideology in Revolutionary America.* New York: W. W. Norton & Company, 1980.

Kilmeade, Brian and Don Yaeger. *George Washington's Secret Six: The Spy Ring That Saved the American Revolution*. New York: Sentinel, 2013.

Koestler-Grack, Rachel A. *Molly Pitcher: Heroine of the War for Independence*. Philadelphia: Chelsea House Publishers, 2006.

Kolchin, Peter. *American Slavery: 1619–1877*. New York: Hill and Wang, 2003.

Lindly, John M. *The History of the Lindley-Lindsley-Linsley Families in America, 1639–1930*. Winfield, IA: Self-Published, 1924.

Lossing, Benson John. *The Pictorial Field-Book of the Revolution*. Vol. 1 and 2. New York: Harper and Brothers, 1850 and 1852.

Lovett, Howard Meriwether. *Grandmother Stories from the Land of Used-to-Be*. Spartanburg, SC: The Reprint Company, 1974.

Martin, Joseph Plumb. *Private Yankee Doodle: Being a Narrative of Some of the Adventures, Dangers, and Sufferings of a Revolutionary Soldier*. Boston: Little, Brown, 1962.

McCall, Hugh. *The History of Georgia, Containing Brief Sketches of the Most Remarkable Events, Up to the Present Day*. Savannah: William T. Williams, 1816.

McCullar, Bernice. *This Is Your Georgia*. Montgomery, AL: Viewpoint Publications, 1968.

McCullough, David G. *1776*. New York: Simon & Schuster, 2005.

McIntosh, John H. *The Official History of Elbert County, 1790–1935*. Athens, GA: The McGregor Company, 1940.

McKnight, Charles. *Our Western Border*. Philadelphia: J. C. McCurdy & Co., 1875.

Meacham, Jon. *American Lion: Andrew Jackson in the White House*. New York: Random House, 2008.

Miner, Ward L. *William Goddard: Newspaperman*. Durham, NC: Duke University Press, 1962.

Monaghan, Charles. *The Murrays of Murray Hill*. Charlottesville, VA: Urban History Press, 1998.

Murray, Sarah. *In the Olden Time: A Short History of the Descendants of John Murray*. New York : Stettiner, Lambert & Co., 1894.

Nash, Gary B. *The Unknown American Revolution*. New York: Viking, 2005.

Northen, William J., ed. *Men of Mark in Georgia*. Vol. 1. Spartanburg, SC: The Reprint Company, 1974.

Odell, Margaretta Matilda. *Memoir and Poems of Phillis Wheatley, a Native African and a Slave*. Boston: I. Knapp, 1838.

Peel, Mrs. William Lawson, ed. *Historical Collections of the Joseph Habersham Chapter, Daughters of the American Revolution*, 1902.

Pennypacker, Morton. *General Washington's Spies on Long Island and in New York*. Brooklyn, NY: The Long Island Historical Society, 1939.

Raphael, Ray. *Founding Myths: Stories That Hide Our Patriotic Past*. New York: New Press, 2004.

———. *A People's History of the American Revolution*. New York: The New Press, 2001.

Redmond, Shirley Raye. *Patriots in Petticoats: Heroines of the American Revolution*. New York: Random House, 2004.

Reed, William B. *Life And Correspondence of Joseph Reed: Military Secretary of Washington, at Cambridge; Adjutant General of the Continental Army; Member of the Congress of the United States; and President of the Executive Council of the State of Pennsylvania*. Vol. 2. Philadelphia: Lindsay and Blakiston, 1847.

Remini, Robert V. *The Life of Andrew Jackson*. New York: Harper & Row, 1988.

Roberts, Cokie. *Founding Mothers: The Women Who Raised Our Nation*. New York: William Morrow, 2004.

Rockwell, Anne. *They Called Her Molly Pitcher*. New York: Alfred A. Knopf, 2002.

Rodgers, Richard. *Rodgers and Hart: A Musical Anthology*. Milwaukee: H. Leonard Pub. Corp., 1995.

Rose, Alexander. *Washington's Spies: The Story of America's First Spy Ring*. New York: Bantam Dell, 2006.

Schecter, Barnet. *The Battle for New York: The City at the Heart of the American Revolution*. New York: Walker & Company, 2002.

Scoggins, Michael C. *The Day It Rained Militia: Huck's Defeat and the Revolution in the South Carolina Backcountry, May–July 1780*. Charleston, SC: The History Press, 2005.

Silcox-Jarrett, Diane. *Heroines of the American Revolution: America's Founding Mothers*. Chapel Hill, NC: Green Angel Press, 1998.

Simms, William Gilmore. *The Life of Francis Marion.* New York: H. G. Langley, 1846.

Somerville, Mollie, compiler. *Women and the American Revolution.* Washington, DC: The National Society, Daughters of the American Revolution, 1974.

Spruill, Marjorie Julian, Valinda A. Littlefield, and Joan Marie Johnson, eds. *South Carolina Women: Their Lives and Times.* Vol. 1. Athens, GA: University of Georgia Press, 2009.

Stone, Clara Jeannette. *Genealogy of the Descendents of Jasper Griffing.* New York: De Baun & Morgenthaler, 1881.

Stryker, William S., author, William Starr Myers, ed. *The Battle of Monmouth.* Princeton, NJ: Princeton University Press, 1927.

Thacher, James, MD. *A Military Journal During the American Revolutionary War, from 1775 to 1783.* Boston: published by Richardson and Lord; printed by J. H. A. Frost, 1823.

Washington Papers, National Archives

Washington, George. Sparks, Jared. *The Writings of George Washington: Correspondence and Miscellaneous Papers Relating to the American Revolution: Boston: Volume VII.* Boston: Ferdinand Andrews, Publisher, 1838.

Watson, John Fanning. *Historic Tales of Olden Time: Concerning the Early Settlement and Progress of Philadelphia and Pennsylvania for the Use of Families and Schools.* Philadelphia: E. Littell and Thomas Holden, 1833.

Weatherford, Doris. *American Women's History.* New York: Prentice Hall General Reference, 1994.

Wheatley, Phillis. *Phillis Wheatley: Complete Writings.* New York: Penguin Books, 2001.

White, Rev. George. *Historical Collections of Georgia.* New York: Pudney & Russell, 1854.

Withers, Alexander Scott. *Chronicles of Border Warfare.* Cincinnati: Robert Clarke Co., 1895.

Worcester, Samuel T. *History of the Town of Hollis, New Hampshire, from Its First Settlement to the Year 1879, with Many Biographical Sketches of Its Early Settlers, Their Descendants, and Other Residents, 1804–1882.* Boston: A. Williams, 1879.

Wright, Louis B. *South Carolina: A Bicentennial History*. New York: Norton, 1976.

Wroth, Lawrence C. *A History of Printing in Colonial Maryland, 1686–1776*. Baltimore: Typothetae of Baltimore, 1922.

———. *The Colonial Printer*. Portland, ME: Southworth-Anthoensen, 1938.

Young, Alfred Fabian. *Masquerade: The Life and Times of Deborah Sampson, Continental Soldier*. New York: Alfred Knopf, 2004.

Zeinert, Karen. *Those Remarkable Women of the American Revolution*. Brookfield, Connecticut: Millbrook Press, 1996.

PLAYS

Sherwood, Robert. *Small War on Murray Hill*. New York: Dramatists Play Service, 1957.

INTERVIEWS

Interview with Peggy Galis. November 18, 2012.

Interviews with Lee Ann Caldwell, Director, Center for the Study of Georgia History, December 5, 2012, and July 3, 2014.

Interviews with Michael Scoggins, Historian, Culture & Heritage Museums, March 1, 2013, and June 2, 2014.

Interview with Douglas Wayne Harvey, West Virginia SAR Historian, July 16, 2014.

Interview with Greg Carroll, Historian (Retired) West Virginia State Archives, September 26, 2014.

DOCUMENTS

Elizabeth Burgin *Letter to Reverend James Calville*, (National Archives Identifier 5916026).

George Washington Papers at the Library of Congress, 1741–1799: Series 4. General Correspondence, 1697–1799.

George Washington Papers at the Library of Congress, 1741–1799: Series 3a, Varick Transcripts.

Hampton, Mrs. Robert. *A Family History*, a handwritten letter, Hargrett Rare Book & Manuscript Library: University of Georgia.

Journals of the Continental Congress, 1774–1789, Volume 20.

Sentiments of An American Woman. Library of Congress.

Sarah Osborn's application for Revolutionary War Pension, Record Camp 15, Records of the Veterans Administration, National Archives, Washington, DC.

MAGAZINES/JOURNALS/PAMPHLETS

Chandler, Ray. "The Legend of Nancy Hart." *North Georgia Journal*, Summer 1999: 22–26.

Coulter, E. Merton. "Nancy Hart, Georgia Heroine of the Revolution: The Story of the Growth of a Tradition." *The Georgia Historical Quarterly* 39, no. 2 (June 1955): 118–51.

Dillard, Richard. "Historic Tea Party of Edenton." *The North Carolina Booklet*. Vol. 23. Raleigh: North Carolina Society of the Revolution, 1926.

Hotchner, William M. "The Scandal Surrounding the Molly Pitcher Overprint Stamp of 1928." *Linn's Stamp News* (August 25, 2008): p. 6.

Marsh, Melinda. "The Purist Patriotism: The Domestic Sphere and the Ladies Association of Philadelphia." (Magazine article included on website: www.history1700s.com)

McMackin, Emily. "Mary Katherine Goddard: Pioneer Printer, Revolutionary Editor." *American Spirit* (March/April 2006): 29–32.

Menkevich, Joseph J. Frankford Chronicles: *Agent Lydia Darragh-Intelligence Operative*. Philadelphia, Pennsylvania (self-published), 2012.

Patrick, Louis S. "Secret Service of the American Revolution." *Connecticut* magazine 11, No. 2, 1907: 265–74.

Shattuck, Mary L. P., *Prudence Wright And The Women Who Guarded The Bridge*, Pepperell, Massachusetts, April, 1775, The Story Of Jewett's Bridge. Ayer, Massachusetts: H. S. Turner, 1912.

Thompson, D. W. and Merri Lou Schaumann. "Goodbye, Molly Pitcher." *Cumberland County History* Vol. 6, no. 1, p. 3–26. (1989).

WEBSITES

History.com
www.history.com/topics/american-revolution

Library of Congress
www.loc.gov

National Archives
www.archives.gov

National Women's History Museum
www.nwhm.org

Museum of the American Revolution
http://amrevmuseum.org/
www.ushistory.org

Index